Shadow Games
How Putin is Undermining America's Global Dominance

Introduction

In the post-Cold War world, the United States stood as the undisputed global superpower, its influence stretching across continents, its ideals championed in every corner of the Earth. But in the shadows of this American dominance, a quiet and calculated challenger has emerged: Vladimir Putin's Russia. Under his leadership, the Russian Federation has been reshaping the global order, deftly maneuvering through political, economic, and military avenues to assert itself as a rival power—one that is not bound by traditional rules, but rather, thrives in the murky spaces of covert influence and hybrid warfare.

Shadow Games explores the sophisticated and strategic methods by which Putin has sought to weaken America's global position. It is a story of power struggles, where traditional notions of diplomacy and warfare have been replaced with cyberattacks, disinformation campaigns, and a calculated effort to exploit the fissures within democratic societies. While the world has largely focused on overt conflicts and military confrontations, this book dives deep into the covert tactics that have allowed Putin to undermine Western institutions, destabilize regions, and erode the very pillars of American influence.

From Russia's covert interventions in Eastern Europe to its rising influence in the Middle East and Asia, Putin's Russia is positioning itself as the new architect of global power. Yet, these efforts are not confined to traditional statecraft alone. In an age where information is as powerful as military might, Russia has embraced cyber warfare and disinformation as critical tools in its arsenal. Whether through tampering with elections or sowing discord among Western allies, the Kremlin's long-term strategy is clear: to chip away at America's global dominance, one shadow game at a time.

This book examines the various facets of Russia's strategy, the intricate and often invisible tactics employed by Putin, and the growing partnership between Russia and China as a counterweight to Western influence. At the heart of this book lies the question of whether America can maintain its position in the face of these emerging challenges. The global chessboard has shifted, and the question is no longer if Russia will succeed in undermining American power, but rather how the United States will respond to the rapidly changing world order.

As we unravel the intricacies of this geopolitical chess game, it is clear that the future of global power will not be determined by military might alone. Instead, it will be shaped by those who can master the art of playing in the shadows—where influence is subtle, power is hidden, and the rules are constantly changing.

Shadow Games is not just a story of international politics, but a stark reminder of the new nature of global power struggles. It challenges us to reconsider what it means to be a superpower in the 21st century and whether America's dominance can withstand the forces working to dismantle it from the inside out.

Chapter 1
The Global Chessboard

The global geopolitical landscape of the 21st century is a complex and constantly shifting puzzle, where power, influence, and strategy are no longer defined by simple territorial control or military might. In this new era, nations play a high-stakes game on a vast chessboard, with alliances, economic power, and information dominance acting as the most critical pieces. For decades, the United States stood at the top of this hierarchy, a global superpower whose decisions resonated worldwide. However, the unipolar world order that America once enjoyed is increasingly under threat, as emerging powers challenge the status quo and old rivalries are reignited. This chapter examines the changing dynamics of global power, where traditional lines are blurred, and the rules of engagement have evolved.

In this high-stakes game, Vladimir Putin's Russia has become a master of playing in the shadows. While the West remains focused on conventional diplomacy and military interventions, Putin has embraced a different strategy: one that exploits the vulnerabilities of modern democracies, uses covert operations to destabilize rival states, and seizes opportunities to expand Russia's influence in strategically critical regions. By manipulating energy resources, harnessing the power of cyber warfare, and aligning with anti-Western factions across the globe, Russia has positioned itself as a formidable player on the world stage. Yet, this is not simply a battle for global dominance; it is a calculated effort to diminish America's influence and undermine its leadership in international affairs.

As the United States faces a new era of competition, the question arises: how does America navigate a world where old rules no longer apply and where power is increasingly decentralized? This chapter sets the stage for understanding the nature of the "Shadow Games" being played by Russia and other rising powers. We will explore the history and evolution of America's position in global politics, Putin's ambitions, and the shifting alliances that challenge traditional models of power. In doing so, we will uncover the intricacies of the new geopolitical landscape and the delicate balance that the United States must maintain in order to preserve its standing in a rapidly changing world order.

The Rise of Modern Geopolitics

The landscape of geopolitics has undergone a profound transformation over the past century. Once dominated by the imperial powers of Europe and later by the two superpowers of the Cold War— the United States and the Soviet Union— the modern geopolitical order is now characterized by a more complex, multipolar world. This shift is a product of several interconnected developments: the decline of colonial empires, the collapse of the Soviet Union, the rise of globalization, and the increasing importance of non-state actors such as multinational corporations, transnational organizations, and, more recently, cyber forces. The new geopolitical environment is defined by competition, uncertainty, and an increasingly interconnected world, where political, economic, and military power is no longer solely in the hands of a few great nations.

Following World War II, the United States emerged as the dominant global power. With the defeat of Nazi Germany and

Imperial Japan, the U.S. solidified its position as the leader of the Western bloc, establishing military alliances like NATO and promoting democratic values through institutions such as the United Nations (UN) and the World Bank. This period marked the beginning of the unipolar moment in world history, with the United States at the helm of a new global order. The U.S. was not only the economic powerhouse but also the leading military force, exerting its influence in the shaping of global trade rules and political structures. This period of American dominance, however, began to wane as new global dynamics took shape.

The Cold War, which divided the world into two opposing camps led by the United States and the Soviet Union, was the most significant geopolitical conflict of the 20th century. This ideological, political, and military rivalry set the stage for many of the global conflicts and alliances that followed. The dissolution of the Soviet Union in 1991, however, marked the end of the bipolar world order and gave rise to a unipolar moment where the U.S. was the sole superpower. This shift was heralded as a new era of global peace, democracy, and capitalist prosperity. But this optimism proved to be short-lived. The collapse of the Soviet Union did not lead to a stable, unified world. Instead, it created a power vacuum and sowed the seeds of new rivalries, especially as regional powers and emerging nations began to assert their influence.

The 21st century has seen the rapid rise of new players on the global stage, most notably China and India. The rapid economic ascent of China, particularly since the 1980s, has shifted the balance of power in Asia and globally. China's aggressive economic policies, technological advancements, and military modernization have made it a formidable challenger to American dominance. Meanwhile, India's growing economy and expanding political influence in international organizations have further altered the geopolitical landscape, making Asia the central hub of global economic and political competition.

In addition to the rise of new powers, the forces of globalization have made traditional geopolitical categories less relevant. Global interconnectedness, driven by advancements in communication and transportation, has blurred the lines between domestic and international politics. Economic interdependence has grown, with global supply chains linking countries that would otherwise have minimal interaction. The rise of the internet and digital technologies has also empowered non-state actors to shape geopolitics. The influence of multinational corporations, NGOs, and even individuals through platforms like social media is now an undeniable force in global affairs. Similarly, cyber threats have emerged as a major element of modern geopolitics, as countries like Russia and China use cyber operations to gain strategic advantage.

The modern geopolitical environment is also heavily influenced by the idea of soft power, a concept championed by American political scientist Joseph Nye. Soft power refers to the ability of a country to influence others through cultural, political, or economic appeal rather than military force. This has been a particularly important area of focus for the U.S., which has used its cultural exports—Hollywood, technology, and consumer brands—as instruments of global influence. However, as new powers like China challenge this dominance, they, too, are leveraging soft power through media, diplomacy, and the promotion of their own values, creating a new form of geopolitical competition.

As the rise of new global powers and the forces of globalization reshape the geopolitical terrain, traditional strategies of statecraft are evolving. The balance of power is becoming increasingly complex, with multiple countries and non-state actors competing for influence. As such, geopolitics in the 21st century is no longer just about military might or economic power—it's about information, technology, and influence. Nations now face the challenge of adapting to a rapidly changing environment, where the lines between war, diplomacy, and competition are no longer clear-cut.

The evolving world of geopolitics has created a stage where traditional players, such as the United States, must adapt to new forms of influence while navigating emerging threats from old rivals. The story of how Russia, under Vladimir Putin, has leveraged these shifts in geopolitics to challenge America's global position is at the heart of understanding the shadow games that are playing out in the current international order.

America's Role as the Global Superpower

Since the end of World War II, the United States has been the cornerstone of global power and influence, assuming a central role in shaping the modern international order. As the only surviving superpower after the war, the U.S. had a unique opportunity to reshape the world in its image, and it did so with remarkable success. The rise of America to global dominance was not merely a consequence of military might; it was the result of a combination of economic strength, democratic ideals, technological innovation, and diplomatic leadership. Over the decades, these elements worked together to solidify America's position as the undisputed leader on the world stage.

One of the primary factors that contributed to America's rise as a global superpower was its economic strength. The U.S. emerged from World War II relatively unscathed, while much of Europe and Asia lay in ruins. This economic advantage allowed the United States to rebuild its economy quickly and decisively. The creation of institutions such as the International Monetary Fund (IMF), the World Bank, and the General Agreement on Tariffs and Trade (GATT) gave the U.S. significant leverage in shaping global economic policies. America's commitment to free markets, capitalism, and liberal democracy helped establish it as the world's leading economic power. The dollar became the de facto global reserve currency, and the U.S. economy became the engine that drove much of the world's growth in the post-war period.

Beyond economics, America's military capabilities also cemented its status as the dominant global power. The U.S. invested heavily in its military during the Cold War, developing a nuclear arsenal that served as both a deterrent and a symbol of its global power. America's military alliances, most notably NATO, allowed it to project its influence across Europe, the Middle East, and Asia. Its dominance in military technology, combined with its leadership in the United Nations and other international institutions, allowed the U.S. to shape global security policies and respond swiftly to emerging threats. Whether through direct military intervention, as in the Korean War or the Gulf War, or through strategic alliances and peacekeeping missions, the U.S. maintained a visible and influential presence around the world.

Diplomatically, the United States played a central role in establishing the institutions that have underpinned the post-World War II order. The U.S. was instrumental in the founding of the United Nations, the World Trade Organization (WTO), and the North Atlantic Treaty Organization (NATO), all of which helped to ensure stability and peace in an increasingly interconnected world. The United States promoted its values of democracy, human rights, and the rule of law, establishing itself as a champion of liberal ideals. This soft power was particularly important during the Cold War, where the U.S. sought to win the ideological battle against the Soviet Union. By promoting democratic governance, free markets, and individual freedoms, the U.S. became the model for much of the Western world and beyond.

Technological and cultural influence also played a pivotal role in America's global dominance. The U.S. has been at the forefront of scientific innovation, from the development of the atomic bomb to the invention of the internet and cutting-edge medical research. These technological advances gave the U.S. a significant edge in both military and civilian domains. American culture, through Hollywood, music, technology, and fashion, also became a global export, helping to spread American ideals and lifestyle across the world. The "American Dream" became a powerful cultural force that attracted people worldwide, further reinforcing America's position as the symbol of opportunity, progress, and modernity.

The geopolitical strategies employed by the United States during the Cold War were also key to its rise as a global superpower. The U.S. sought to contain the spread of communism, primarily through military alliances and foreign aid programs, such as the Marshall Plan, which helped rebuild Western Europe after World War II. America's involvement in global conflicts, from the Korean and Vietnam Wars to the more recent wars in the Middle East, was driven by its desire to prevent the expansion of Soviet influence and maintain a balance of power favorable to Western interests. This policy of containment, coupled with the strategic use of soft power and military might, allowed the U.S. to maintain its global leadership throughout much of the 20th century.

However, the post-Cold War era has brought new challenges to America's position as the undisputed global superpower. While the U.S. remains the dominant military force and the largest economy, rising powers such as China and Russia have increasingly sought to challenge its hegemony. The economic rise of China, in particular, has led to a more multipolar world, where the U.S. must share influence with other global players. Additionally, the rise of non-state actors, such as transnational corporations and terrorist organizations, has made it more difficult for any one nation to exercise complete control over global affairs.

Nevertheless, America's role as the global superpower is far from over. The United States continues to wield immense influence through its military presence, economic clout, and cultural power. Yet, the world is changing, and the U.S. must adapt to a new era of global competition. This chapter explores America's historical trajectory as the global superpower, examining the factors that helped it rise to prominence and the challenges it faces in maintaining that status in a rapidly evolving world order. As we will see, the shifting tides of geopolitics will test America's ability to retain its leadership role, especially in the face of emerging powers and the complex, interconnected global challenges of the 21st century.

The Shadow of Russia's Strategic Intentions

Russia's strategic intentions on the global stage are often shrouded in mystery and calculated ambiguity. Under the leadership of Vladimir Putin, Russia has navigated a complex course, employing a combination of military power, cyber warfare, economic influence, and political subversion to reclaim its status as a dominant global player. Unlike the overt tactics of traditional powers, Russia has mastered the art of working from the shadows, using asymmetric methods to challenge the West and undermine global stability in ways that are not always immediately apparent. Understanding Russia's true strategic objectives requires delving into the historical, political, and ideological drivers that have shaped its current actions on the world stage.

At the heart of Russia's strategic intentions lies the desire to reassert itself as a great power, reclaiming its former Soviet glory and counteracting what it perceives as a western encroachment on its sphere of influence. The collapse of the Soviet Union in 1991 was a profound blow to Russia's status and national pride. For Putin and many within Russia's ruling elite, the disintegration of the USSR is viewed as a traumatic event—a geopolitical catastrophe that left Russia isolated and weakened. Putin has consistently expressed his desire to restore Russia's power, albeit not through the same ideological apparatus that governed the Soviet Union. Rather, he has focused on rebuilding Russia's influence through a blend of nationalism, authoritarian governance, and pragmatic foreign policy.

Putin's strategic approach is largely driven by the need to secure Russia's borders and establish a sphere of influence in the former Soviet republics, particularly in Eastern Europe and Central Asia. Russia views NATO's expansion as a direct threat to its security and a violation of agreements made at the end of the Cold War. As a result, Putin's government has taken aggressive steps to maintain influence over countries like Ukraine, Belarus, and Georgia, which were once part of the Soviet Union. The annexation of Crimea in 2014 was a clear demonstration of Russia's determination to reclaim lost territory and reassert its dominance in its near abroad. The Kremlin's involvement in the conflict in Eastern Ukraine, coupled with its support for separatist movements in other former Soviet states, is part of a broader effort to maintain political and military influence in the region and prevent Western powers from gaining a foothold in what Russia considers its backyard.

In addition to territorial ambitions, Russia's broader strategy includes an effort to weaken and destabilize Western democracies. Cyber warfare and information operations have become key tools in Putin's geopolitical playbook. The Russian government has been linked to a series of cyberattacks and disinformation campaigns aimed at undermining the stability of Western nations, most notably the United States and European Union. The hacking of political institutions, interference in elections, and the spread of fake news and propaganda are all part of a coordinated effort to sow discord within these countries, erode public trust in their institutions, and create divisions that Russia can exploit. This use of non-traditional warfare, often referred to as "hybrid warfare," allows Russia to challenge Western powers without engaging in direct military conflict, making it a cost-effective way to achieve strategic objectives while avoiding the risks of open warfare.

Russia's global ambitions also extend to challenging the international liberal order that the United States and its allies have built since World War II. Putin views this order—characterized by institutions such as the United Nations, the World Trade Organization, and the International Monetary Fund—as an instrument of Western dominance that restricts Russia's ability to pursue its national interests. In response, Russia has sought to weaken these institutions, either by undermining their legitimacy or by bypassing them entirely. Putin has worked to cultivate alliances with other authoritarian regimes, such as China and Iran, in a bid to create an alternative to the liberal international order. This aligns with his vision of a multipolar world where Russia can play a leading role, not as a subordinate to the West, but as an equal and influential power.

Another key element of Russia's strategic intentions is the use of energy as a tool of geopolitical leverage. Russia is one of the world's largest producers and exporters of oil and natural gas, and its control over energy resources gives it significant influence over European countries that depend on Russian energy supplies. By using its position as a major energy supplier, Russia has the ability to exert pressure on its neighbors and the European Union, sometimes using energy cutoffs as a political weapon to achieve its strategic goals. This economic leverage extends beyond Europe, with Russia engaging in energy deals with countries in Asia and the Middle East to strengthen its global influence and reduce its dependence on Western markets.

Despite these aggressive strategies, Russia remains acutely aware of its vulnerabilities. Its economy is heavily dependent on energy exports, and it faces internal challenges such as demographic decline, corruption, and political unrest. Furthermore, while Russia seeks to assert its global influence, it remains cautious about direct military confrontations with the West, particularly given the nuclear deterrence capabilities possessed by both Russia and the United States. Instead, Russia has chosen to play the long game, using a variety of tools to undermine its adversaries while avoiding the risks of open conflict.

In conclusion, Russia's strategic intentions are centered around a desire to restore its global influence and status as a great power. Through a combination of territorial expansion, hybrid warfare, alliances with authoritarian regimes, and the use of energy resources, Russia seeks to challenge Western dominance and create a new multipolar world order. These intentions are deeply rooted in historical grievances, national pride, and a desire to protect Russia's sovereignty from what it perceives as the encroachment of Western powers. As Russia continues to expand its reach and influence, its strategic moves will undoubtedly shape the future of global geopolitics, especially as it seeks to counterbalance the dominance of the United States and its allies.

Chapter 2
The Putin Doctrine

Vladimir Putin's rise to power in Russia marked the beginning of a new era in the country's foreign policy, one that would prioritize national sovereignty, geopolitical influence, and the reassertion of Russia's global power. The "Putin Doctrine" represents a strategic framework that has been built upon a blend of historical Russian imperial ambitions, the trauma of the Soviet Union's collapse, and a relentless drive to challenge the West. At its core, the Putin Doctrine seeks to elevate Russia to the status of a major global player, counteracting what the Kremlin sees as an ongoing western encroachment into its sphere of influence. It blends military force, strategic alliances, economic leverage, and information warfare into a multifaceted approach that aims to reshape the global order in Russia's favor.

A key aspect of the Putin Doctrine is the rejection of a unipolar world dominated by the United States. Putin's Russia seeks to establish a multipolar world, where power is distributed among various regional and global powers, including Russia, China, and other emerging economies. This vision is deeply rooted in Russia's historical narrative, where it sees itself not just as a regional power but as a global force capable of balancing Western influence. The doctrine emphasizes Russia's right to exert its power and influence within its own backyard, particularly in Eastern Europe, the Caucasus, and Central Asia. In this view, NATO's expansion and the spread of liberal democratic values are perceived as existential threats to Russia's national security, and Putin's foreign policy has been largely shaped by the need to safeguard Russia's borders from what he views as hostile Western encroachment.

The Putin Doctrine is also characterized by the use of asymmetric warfare and hybrid tactics. Unlike the conventional warfare strategies of the past, Putin's Russia has pioneered the use of cyberattacks, disinformation campaigns, and economic sanctions as tools of statecraft. These methods allow Russia to challenge its adversaries, particularly the United States and the European Union, without engaging in direct military conflict. The doctrine's reliance on information warfare, in particular, has been a significant feature of Putin's approach, as seen in the cyberattacks on Western democracies, interference in elections, and the propagation of propaganda through state-controlled media outlets. By leveraging these non-traditional tactics, Russia is able to destabilize its opponents and reshape global narratives without the need for conventional military engagement, making the Putin Doctrine both highly effective and highly elusive in its execution.

In essence, the Putin Doctrine represents Russia's strategic response to a rapidly changing global order. It is a doctrine rooted in both history and pragmatism, seeking to protect Russia's sovereignty while reclaiming its place as a dominant force on the world stage. As Russia continues to execute this doctrine through a blend of traditional and non-traditional means, it challenges Western values and power structures, demanding a reevaluation of the rules that have governed international relations since the end of the Cold War. This chapter will explore the key tenets of the Putin Doctrine, examining how they have shaped Russian foreign policy and how they continue to influence global geopolitics today.

Putin's Vision for Russia

Vladimir Putin's vision for Russia is deeply rooted in a desire to restore the country's status as a global power while safeguarding its sovereignty and national pride. For Putin, the collapse of the Soviet Union in 1991 was not merely the end of an ideological system; it was a geopolitical catastrophe that left Russia weakened, fragmented, and humiliated. The aftermath of the USSR's dissolution created a power vacuum in which Russia found itself diminished on the world stage, both politically and economically. From the moment he took power in 1999, Putin has made it his mission to reverse this decline, rebuild Russia's international stature, and recapture the influence it once wielded as a superpower.

At the core of Putin's vision is the restoration of Russia's dominance in its traditional sphere of influence, particularly in Eastern Europe, Central Asia, and the former Soviet republics. He believes that Russia has a natural right to exert control and influence over these regions, and any Western interference is seen as a direct threat to the country's security. This vision is grounded in Russia's historical identity as both an empire and a major global power, and it draws upon the notion of a "greater Russia" that extends beyond its current borders. Putin's policies in Ukraine, Georgia, and Moldova reflect this strategic priority, as he has worked to assert Russian control over these territories, using a mix of military force, covert operations, and diplomatic pressure to ensure that these states remain within Russia's orbit or under its influence. The annexation of Crimea in 2014, followed by military support for separatist movements in Eastern Ukraine, exemplifies Putin's willingness to employ force when necessary to preserve what he views as Russia's rightful sphere of influence.

Putin's vision for Russia is also strongly tied to the idea of restoring national pride and political stability within the country. Under his leadership, Russia has moved away from the chaotic years of the 1990s, which were marked by economic collapse, widespread corruption, and a loss of national identity. Putin has emphasized the importance of a strong, centralized government capable of restoring order, enforcing the rule of law, and curbing the influence of oligarchs and political elites. This has led to the creation of a system that blends authoritarian rule with a managed democracy, where opposition is suppressed, media freedom is restricted, and political dissent is often met with harsh repression. By consolidating power within the Kremlin and limiting political competition, Putin has been able to maintain a firm grip on Russia's governance, projecting an image of strength and stability both domestically and internationally.

Economically, Putin has sought to modernize Russia's economy while reducing its dependency on Western powers. He has worked to create economic partnerships with other countries, particularly in Asia, in order to diversify Russia's economic ties and reduce reliance on Europe and the United States. Russia's vast natural resources, particularly its oil and natural gas reserves, have been central to this strategy. Putin has used energy exports as both a source of wealth and a tool of geopolitical leverage, particularly over European nations that rely on Russian energy. However, despite the growth of Russia's energy sector, Putin's vision for the future of Russia's economy also includes efforts to develop other industries, such as technology and manufacturing, in order to make Russia more self-sufficient and less vulnerable to fluctuations in global commodity markets.

On the global stage, Putin's vision includes the creation of a multipolar world where Russia plays a central role in counterbalancing the dominance of the United States and its Western allies. Russia's foreign policy under Putin has been defined by a strong anti-Western stance, driven by a belief that Western powers seek to undermine Russia's sovereignty and impose their values on the world. Putin views NATO expansion, the spread of liberal democracy, and Western economic sanctions as direct threats to Russia's security and autonomy. In response, he has sought to strengthen alliances with other non-Western powers, particularly China, while also working to weaken Western institutions from within. Russia's involvement in the Syrian Civil War, its support for anti-Western governments in Venezuela and Iran, and its efforts to disrupt democratic processes in the U.S. and Europe through cyberattacks and disinformation campaigns are all part of Putin's broader strategy to challenge the liberal international order and shift the balance of global power in favor of Russia and its allies.

Putin's vision for Russia is also rooted in a desire to preserve and promote Russian culture and values, which he believes are under threat from the forces of globalization, secularism, and Western influence. This aspect of his vision is tied to his concept of Russian exceptionalism, which asserts that Russia has a unique cultural and spiritual identity that sets it apart from the West. Putin has positioned himself as a defender of traditional Russian values, particularly in contrast to the liberal social policies of the West. This has been reflected in his support for conservative causes, such as opposition to same-sex marriage and his emphasis on the role of the Russian Orthodox Church in public life. By championing these values, Putin aims to cultivate a sense of national unity and pride, while appealing to the conservative segments of Russian society.

In conclusion, Putin's vision for Russia is multifaceted, combining geopolitical ambition, economic modernization, political consolidation, and cultural revival. At its heart, this vision is driven by a desire to restore Russia's global power and influence, particularly in the former Soviet territories, while countering the perceived threats from the West. Putin's strategy is pragmatic, relying on a mixture of military power, economic leverage, political control, and soft power to achieve his goals. Whether or not this vision will secure Russia's place as a global power in the 21st century remains uncertain, but it has undeniably reshaped the geopolitical landscape and posed significant challenges to the United States and its allies.

Rebuilding Russia's Power and Influence

Vladimir Putin's tenure has been defined by a singular goal: the restoration of Russia's global power and influence. After the collapse of the Soviet Union in 1991, Russia faced a profound crisis of national identity and geopolitical stature. The disintegration of the USSR marked the end of an era in which Russia had been one of the world's two superpowers. Under Boris Yeltsin's leadership in the 1990s, Russia experienced a period of instability marked by economic turmoil, political chaos, and a loss of global standing. However, Putin's rise to power in 1999 heralded the beginning of an effort to rebuild Russia's position on the world stage, both regionally and globally. His strategy has involved consolidating domestic power, modernizing the military, and employing a mix of diplomacy, energy leverage, and military interventions to regain Russia's influence in key regions and challenge the West.

One of the foundational elements of Putin's strategy for rebuilding Russia's power has been the restoration of internal political stability and centralization of authority. The chaotic post-Soviet years left Russia vulnerable to both internal and external threats, as regional elites wielded considerable power, and the state's control over its resources was fragmented. Putin moved quickly to reassert control over the country's vast resources, particularly its energy sector, and to consolidate power within the Kremlin. Through a combination of political maneuvering, silencing of opposition, and selective use of state power, Putin created a tightly controlled political system that prioritized national unity and order. This centralized control allowed him to implement his strategic objectives with greater efficiency, making it easier to project power abroad and manage domestic dissent.

A crucial element of Putin's strategy for rebuilding Russia's power has been the modernization and expansion of Russia's military capabilities. After the dissolution of the Soviet Union, Russia inherited a vast nuclear arsenal but lacked the financial and logistical means to maintain or upgrade its conventional military forces. In the early years of Putin's presidency, Russia's military was in disrepair, and its ability to project power beyond its borders was limited. Putin, however, made it a priority to overhaul Russia's military, increasing defense spending and investing in advanced weaponry, including modernized tanks, fighter jets, and naval assets. The focus was not only on rebuilding conventional forces but also on enhancing Russia's nuclear deterrent, which remains a cornerstone of its defense posture. This military modernization allowed Russia to reclaim a significant portion of its former military influence and to intervene decisively in regional conflicts, most notably in Georgia (2008) and Ukraine (2014).

Putin's military assertiveness in these conflicts also serves as a demonstration of Russia's renewed geopolitical ambitions. The invasion of Georgia in 2008 and the annexation of Crimea in 2014 were clear signals to both the West and Russia's neighbors that Moscow would not tolerate Western encroachment in what it considers its sphere of influence. The actions in Crimea, particularly, were framed by Putin as a necessary move to protect Russian-speaking populations and to prevent Ukraine from aligning with NATO, an alliance that Russia views as a direct threat to its security. These interventions, though costly in terms of international relations, have served to reinforce Russia's position in its near abroad, while sending a broader message that Russia is willing to assert its interests militarily when necessary.

In addition to military power, Putin has used Russia's energy resources as a critical tool in rebuilding its geopolitical influence. Russia is one of the world's largest producers of oil and natural gas, and it has long used its energy wealth to exert influence over Europe, particularly in countries that rely heavily on Russian energy exports. Putin has strategically used Russia's energy exports as both a source of revenue and a geopolitical weapon. By controlling natural gas pipelines that run through Ukraine, Belarus, and other Eastern European nations, Russia has been able to exert leverage over these countries, cutting off supplies when they align too closely with the West or NATO. Additionally, Russia has worked to diversify its energy export markets, entering into long-term deals with China and other Asian nations to reduce its reliance on Europe.

Diplomatically, Putin has sought to rebuild Russia's influence by strengthening relationships with non-Western powers, particularly in the Middle East and Asia. Russia's intervention in Syria, where it has supported the regime of Bashar al-Assad, has marked a return to the Middle East as a key area of influence for Russia. Through its military and diplomatic engagement, Russia has positioned itself as a counterbalance to U.S. influence in the region, fostering alliances with countries such as Iran, Turkey, and Hezbollah. These alliances, though sometimes fraught with complexity, have allowed Russia to assert itself as a regional power capable of shaping the outcomes of conflicts in its favor.

At the same time, Russia has cultivated a strategic partnership with China, which has become an increasingly important element of its foreign policy. The economic and military ties between Russia and China have strengthened over the years, with both countries sharing a common interest in countering U.S. dominance. The Russia-China relationship is based on mutual benefit, with China seeking to secure energy supplies from Russia and Russia looking to tap into China's growing economy and technological expertise. This partnership has allowed Russia to circumvent some of the economic sanctions imposed by the West, while simultaneously strengthening its position on the global stage.

Putin's efforts to rebuild Russia's power and influence have not been without significant challenges. Russia's economy, while large, remains overly dependent on energy exports, leaving it vulnerable to fluctuations in global commodity prices. Additionally, Russia's actions in Ukraine and its involvement in Syria have led to strained relations with the West, resulting in sanctions that have further isolated the country economically. Nevertheless, Putin's strategic vision has succeeded in re-establishing Russia as a major global player, capable of challenging the United States and Europe in various spheres of influence. As Russia continues to assert its position in global affairs, its ability to leverage military power, energy resources, and strategic alliances will remain key factors in its bid to reshape the geopolitical order.

The Kremlin's Long-Term Global Strategy

The Kremlin's long-term global strategy is centered around restoring Russia's status as a dominant world power, reversing the humiliation it experienced following the collapse of the Soviet Union, and safeguarding its sovereignty from perceived Western encroachment. Vladimir Putin's administration has pursued a multifaceted approach to achieving these objectives, blending military force, strategic alliances, economic leverage, and information warfare to strengthen Russia's position globally. The overarching goal of this strategy is not only to reassert Russia's power in its immediate sphere of influence but also to challenge the liberal international order, which the Kremlin views as a construct that primarily serves Western interests, particularly those of the United States and its European allies.

One of the central pillars of the Kremlin's long-term strategy is the restoration of Russia's geopolitical influence over its near abroad, especially in the former Soviet republics. These regions are seen as critical to Russia's national security and its quest to regain the status of a global power. The Kremlin's approach to these territories has been consistent: maintain control through political influence, military intervention, and economic leverage. Russia's actions in Ukraine, including the annexation of Crimea in 2014 and its ongoing involvement in the Donbas region, are prime examples of the Kremlin's willingness to use military force to preserve its strategic interests. The Kremlin also seeks to maintain influence over countries such as Georgia, Moldova, and Armenia, where Russia has a strong military presence, political influence, and economic ties. Through alliances like the Collective Security Treaty Organization (CSTO) and organizations like the Eurasian Economic Union (EEU), the Kremlin aims to create a bloc of states that will be economically and politically aligned with Russia, thus reinforcing its leadership in the region and preventing Western encroachment, especially from NATO.

The Kremlin's long-term strategy also hinges on undermining the global liberal order led by the United States and the European Union. Putin and other Russian officials view the post-Cold War international system, characterized by democratic norms, free-market capitalism, and the expansion of Western institutions like NATO and the European Union, as a threat to Russia's sovereignty and influence. Russia's actions in this regard are both strategic and ideological. The Kremlin has worked to destabilize the international order by challenging Western democratic values and promoting alternative governance models. This includes fostering relationships with authoritarian regimes, such as China, Iran, and Venezuela, that share Russia's skepticism toward Western democracy. Russia's efforts to weaken or bypass Western-dominated international institutions, like the United Nations and the World Trade Organization, are also part of this strategy. By challenging these organizations and fostering alliances with non-Western powers, the Kremlin aims to create a multipolar world order where Russia plays a central role, counterbalancing the U.S. and its allies.

In addition to its regional ambitions and opposition to the Western liberal order, Russia has increasingly relied on asymmetric warfare, particularly in the domains of cyberattacks and disinformation, as a key component of its long-term strategy. In recent years, Russia has used these tools not only to protect its interests but also to destabilize adversaries. The Kremlin's cyber capabilities are advanced, and it has employed them to interfere in foreign elections, disrupt critical infrastructure, and influence public opinion in countries like the United States, the United Kingdom, and across Europe. The Russian government's involvement in disinformation campaigns has been an essential part of this strategy, using state-controlled media, social media bots, and false narratives to sow division and confusion within Western democracies. By engaging in these covert activities, Russia can exert influence without resorting to traditional military intervention, which helps it avoid direct confrontation with the West while still achieving its strategic goals.

Energy resources also remain a cornerstone of Russia's long-term global strategy. As one of the world's largest producers of oil and natural gas, Russia uses its energy exports as both an economic driver and a tool of geopolitical leverage. The Kremlin has employed energy as a weapon by using its control over key pipelines to exert influence over Europe, which relies heavily on Russian gas supplies. The construction of new pipelines like Nord Stream 2, which bypasses Ukraine and directly connects Russia to Germany, is part of the Kremlin's strategy to solidify its hold over Europe's energy markets and further isolate Ukraine. By using energy resources to influence European policy, Russia aims to deepen divisions within the European Union and weaken its unity, especially in relation to NATO and sanctions against Russia.

Russia's strategy also includes a focus on military modernization, particularly in areas that could counter Western military superiority. The Kremlin has invested heavily in developing advanced weapons systems, including nuclear-capable missile technology, hypersonic missiles, and new generations of tanks, aircraft, and submarines. These investments are designed to ensure that Russia can maintain a credible military deterrent, particularly against NATO, while also asserting its influence in regions like the Arctic and the Middle East. In recent years, Russia's military interventions in Syria and its involvement in other global hotspots have underscored its intent to project power beyond its borders, ensuring that it remains a key player in shaping global security dynamics.

Russia's foreign policy is also characterized by efforts to foster closer ties with China, its most significant strategic partner in the 21st century. As both Russia and China share common interests in countering U.S. global dominance, they have deepened their military, economic, and political cooperation. Through initiatives like the Shanghai Cooperation Organization (SCO) and the Belt and Road Initiative (BRI), Russia and China aim to create an alternative economic and security architecture that challenges Western influence. The growing partnership between Russia and China further solidifies the Kremlin's global strategy by providing it with a powerful ally in the Asia-Pacific region, enabling Russia to exert pressure on the West from multiple fronts.

In conclusion, the Kremlin's long-term global strategy is built around several core objectives: reasserting Russia's dominance in its near abroad, undermining the liberal international order, utilizing energy resources and military power to influence global affairs, and fostering strategic alliances with non-Western powers. By combining traditional military tactics with modern methods of asymmetric warfare, Russia seeks to challenge the West without engaging in direct military confrontation, effectively shifting the global balance of power in its favor. As Putin continues to navigate these complex challenges, the Kremlin's long-term strategy remains a critical factor in shaping the future of global geopolitics.

Chapter 3
The Battle for Influence in Eastern Europe

Eastern Europe has long been a region of strategic importance, acting as both a buffer zone and a battleground for competing global powers. During the Cold War, it was firmly within the Soviet sphere of influence, with nations such as Poland, Hungary, and the Czech Republic governed by pro-Soviet regimes. However, the fall of the Berlin Wall in 1989 and the subsequent collapse of the Soviet Union in 1991 fundamentally reshaped the geopolitical landscape of the region. As Eastern European countries transitioned to democracy and market economies, they sought to align themselves more closely with the West, particularly with the European Union (EU) and NATO. This shift presented a direct challenge to Russia, which viewed the growing influence of Western institutions as a threat to its historical dominance over the region.

For Vladimir Putin's Russia, the loss of Eastern Europe to the West was a bitter blow, and since coming to power in 1999, Putin has made it clear that he intends to regain Russia's influence in the region. He views the expansion of NATO and the EU into Eastern Europe as a strategic encroachment on Russia's security and a direct challenge to its authority. Russia's response has been multifaceted, combining military intervention, political pressure, and economic leverage to maintain influence over countries in the region that have historical, cultural, and political ties to Russia. The Kremlin has sought to destabilize the political environments of these countries, sometimes through overt force, as seen in Georgia in 2008 and Ukraine in 2014, and other times through more subtle means, such as disinformation campaigns, economic sanctions, and fostering political divisions.

The battle for influence in Eastern Europe is not just about territorial control; it is about the ideological and strategic alignment of nations at the crossroads of Europe and Russia. As Russia seeks to challenge NATO's eastern expansion and the EU's growing influence, it faces opposition from both Western powers and the governments of many Eastern European states that view their future within the frameworks of the EU and NATO. These countries are caught in a precarious position, torn between the allure of Western economic and security integration and the pressures from Moscow to remain within Russia's orbit. The conflict over influence in Eastern Europe is a microcosm of the broader global struggle for power and control between Russia and the West, one that will continue to shape the future of the region and international relations as a whole. This chapter explores how Russia has sought to reclaim its influence in Eastern Europe, the methods it has employed, and the challenges it faces in an increasingly divided and complex geopolitical environment.

Ukraine: The Heart of the Conflict

Ukraine has long been a focal point of geopolitical struggle, caught between the historical spheres of influence of Russia and the West. Its strategic location, vast natural resources, and importance as a transit route for energy supplies have made it a vital piece in the global power game. For Russia, Ukraine holds immense symbolic and strategic value, not only because of its proximity but also due to the deep historical, cultural, and political ties between the two nations.

However, Ukraine's desire for greater integration with the European Union (EU) and its aspirations to join NATO have put it at odds with Moscow, sparking one of the most intense and prolonged conflicts in the post-Soviet era.

The conflict over Ukraine's future began to escalate in 2013, when the then-Ukrainian President Viktor Yanukovych, under pressure from Russia, abandoned an association agreement with the European Union in favor of closer ties with Moscow. This decision sparked massive protests, known as the Euromaidan movement, as many Ukrainians, particularly in the western part of the country, saw the move as a betrayal of their pro-European aspirations. The protests ultimately led to Yanukovych's ousting in February 2014, a change of government that Russia saw as a threat to its strategic interests. Putin's government viewed the political upheaval in Ukraine as a Western-backed coup and responded with a swift military intervention. In March 2014, Russia annexed Crimea, a move that was condemned by the international community and marked the beginning of the ongoing conflict in Ukraine.

Crimea's annexation was a bold demonstration of Russia's willingness to use military force to protect its interests in Ukraine. For Russia, Crimea holds immense strategic significance due to its location on the Black Sea and the presence of Russia's Black Sea Fleet in Sevastopol. The annexation not only secured Russia's military foothold in the region but also sent a clear message to the West: Moscow would not tolerate any movement by Ukraine towards greater integration with NATO or the EU. In addition to Crimea, Russia also supported separatist movements in the Donbas region of eastern Ukraine, where pro-Russian militants, backed by Russian troops, declared independence in the self-proclaimed republics of Donetsk and Luhansk. This conflict, often referred to as the Russo-

Ukrainian War, has led to thousands of deaths and the displacement of millions of people, creating a frozen conflict that remains unresolved.

The war in Ukraine is not merely a territorial dispute; it is emblematic of the broader struggle between Russia and the West for influence in Eastern Europe. Putin's actions in Ukraine reflect his broader geopolitical vision, which seeks to reassert Russian dominance in the region and counter the expanding influence of NATO and the EU. Ukraine, as the largest and most strategically important of the post-Soviet states, has become the heart of this struggle. Moscow views Ukraine's potential membership in NATO as a direct threat to its security, as it would place a Western military alliance on Russia's borders. For the West, Ukraine represents a test case for the post-Cold War order, where countries should be free to choose their own alliances and pursue economic and political integration without fear of coercion from neighboring powers.

Ukraine's desire to move closer to the West has been further fueled by the widespread corruption and mismanagement that characterized much of its post-Soviet governance. Many Ukrainians, particularly those in the western and central regions, see European integration as a path to economic modernization, democratic reform, and greater stability. The 2014 Euromaidan protests, which were sparked by opposition to Yanukovych's pro-Russian policies, were not only about foreign policy but also about the desire for a more transparent, accountable government. As the conflict has continued, Ukraine has increasingly looked to the West for support, seeking economic aid, military assistance, and diplomatic backing from NATO and the EU. This shift toward the West has further angered Russia, which views Ukraine's pro-European direction as a betrayal of its historical ties and a threat to its regional ambitions.

The international response to the conflict has been mixed. While the West has imposed sanctions on Russia and provided varying levels of support to Ukraine, NATO has been reluctant to directly intervene, partly due to fears of escalating the conflict into a broader war with Russia. The European Union has also offered Ukraine financial assistance and political support, but the long road to full EU membership remains uncertain. The Minsk Agreements, signed in 2015, aimed at de-escalating the conflict, have failed to bring about a lasting peace, and fighting continues sporadically in eastern Ukraine. The ongoing war has left Ukraine deeply divided, with a significant portion of the population in the eastern and southern regions still sympathetic to Russia, while the western and central parts of the country have moved decisively toward integration with the European Union.

The conflict in Ukraine is ultimately about more than just territorial control—it is a reflection of competing visions for the future of Eastern Europe. Russia's vision, under Putin's leadership, is one of a strong, resurgent Russia that dominates its neighbors, while the West's vision is one of democratic expansion and the free choice of alliances. Ukraine's future remains uncertain, but its struggle is central to the larger battle for influence in Eastern Europe. The outcome of this conflict will have profound implications not only for Ukraine but for the entire region, as it will determine the balance of power between Russia and the West in one of the most strategically important areas of the world.

Russian Influence in Moldova and Georgia

Moldova and Georgia, two former Soviet republics situated at the crossroads of Europe and Asia, have long been in the orbit of Russian geopolitical influence. Despite their aspirations to move closer to the European Union (EU) and NATO, both countries have struggled with Russia's political, economic, and military pressure, which has played a significant role in shaping their domestic and foreign policies. Russia's influence in Moldova and Georgia is driven by a combination of strategic, cultural, and historical factors, which the Kremlin has leveraged to maintain a dominant position in the region and prevent these nations from fully integrating with Western institutions.

Moldova, one of the poorest countries in Europe, has been particularly vulnerable to Russian influence since gaining independence in 1991. The country's internal divisions, ethnic composition, and economic dependencies have made it an attractive target for Russian influence. Moldova's breakaway region, Transnistria, which borders Ukraine, has been a focal point of Russian intervention. Since the early 1990s, following Moldova's declaration of independence from the Soviet Union, Transnistria declared itself an independent republic, though it has never been recognized internationally. With a significant Russian-speaking population, Transnistria has remained heavily dependent on Russia for political, economic, and military support. Russian military forces continue to maintain a presence in the region under the guise of peacekeeping, further complicating Moldova's sovereignty and its efforts to forge closer ties with the West.

Russia's strategic interest in Moldova lies in its desire to maintain a buffer zone between NATO and Russia's borders, as well as its historical ties to the region. For Putin's government, Moldova is a key part of the "near abroad" — the former Soviet republics that Russia views as within its sphere of influence. To prevent Moldova from fully aligning with the EU and NATO, Russia has used a variety of tools to weaken pro-Western political movements. These tactics have included leveraging Moldova's dependence on Russian energy supplies, engaging in economic coercion, and supporting pro-Russian political factions in Moldova. Moscow has also worked to undermine Moldova's European integration efforts by offering economic incentives to Moldovan politicians who support closer ties with Russia, while using its influence over the breakaway region of Transnistria to destabilize Moldova's political environment.

In recent years, Moldova's government has alternated between pro-European and pro-Russian leadership, often resulting in political instability and public disillusionment. Russia's involvement has exacerbated Moldova's internal divisions, with a significant portion of the population, especially in the breakaway region and the Russian-speaking east, leaning towards Moscow. Despite these challenges, Moldova has continued to pursue an EU integration path, culminating in the signing of an Association Agreement with the EU in 2014. However, the country's internal fractures, compounded by Russian pressure, make Moldova's journey toward full European integration uncertain and fraught with difficulties.

Georgia, like Moldova, has faced a similar struggle with Russian influence since gaining independence after the collapse of the Soviet Union. However, Georgia's situation is more complicated due to its strategic location in the Caucasus region, which serves as a critical transit route for energy and trade between Europe and Asia. The Kremlin has long seen Georgia as an important part of its regional sphere of influence and has made every effort to maintain control over the country, using a combination of military intervention, political manipulation, and economic coercion.

One of the most significant flashpoints between Georgia and Russia occurred in the early 2000s, particularly with the conflicts over the regions of Abkhazia and South Ossetia. Both of these regions, located within Georgia's internationally recognized borders, declared independence following the dissolution of the Soviet Union, but were never recognized by the international community. In 2008, after Georgia moved toward NATO integration and signed an agreement with the United States, Russia responded with a military intervention in both regions, leading to the Russo-Georgian War. The conflict ended with a ceasefire brokered by the French presidency, but it resulted in Russia's recognition of both Abkhazia and South Ossetia as independent republics. Russian military forces have since maintained a significant presence in these territories, further solidifying their de facto control.

Russia's role in Abkhazia and South Ossetia is part of its broader strategy to prevent Georgia from joining NATO or forming closer ties with the EU. The Kremlin views Georgia's potential NATO membership as a direct threat to its security and regional dominance. By maintaining military forces in Georgia's breakaway regions, Russia has not only prevented Georgia's full integration into Western institutions but has also destabilized the country politically. These frozen conflicts have created a situation in which Georgia must constantly navigate its foreign policy between the pressure of maintaining sovereignty over its disputed territories and the desire to integrate with Western institutions.

At the same time, Russia has leveraged its energy resources and trade to maintain economic influence over Georgia. Moscow has repeatedly used economic sanctions as a tool to punish Georgia for its pro-Western policies, particularly after the 2008 war. The Kremlin's ability to restrict trade and cut off energy supplies has made Georgia's economic position precarious, reinforcing its dependency on Russia. However, Georgia has actively sought to diversify its economic partnerships, particularly with the EU and the United States, in an effort to reduce its dependence on Russia.

Despite Russia's continued efforts to undermine Georgia's sovereignty, the country has made significant strides in its pursuit of European integration. Georgia signed an Association Agreement with the EU in 2014, and its citizens were granted visa-free access to the Schengen Area in 2017. Georgia's NATO aspirations remain a central element of its foreign policy, though the ongoing conflicts in Abkhazia and South Ossetia continue to complicate its relationship with the alliance.

Russia's influence in Moldova and Georgia is deeply intertwined with its broader regional and global strategy. Both countries have been caught in a tug-of-war between Russia's desire to maintain its sphere of influence and their aspirations for closer ties with the West. While Moldova and Georgia continue to resist Russian pressure, both nations face significant internal and external challenges that make their future integration into European and transatlantic structures uncertain. As Russia continues to employ a mix of military intervention, political manipulation, and economic leverage to assert its control, the future of Moldova and Georgia will remain crucial to the geopolitical dynamics of Eastern Europe and the Caucasus. Russia's actions in these countries underscore its determination to keep its former Soviet territories within its orbit, preventing them from becoming fully integrated into the Western sphere.

NATO Expansion and its Repercussions

Since its establishment in 1949, the North Atlantic Treaty Organization (NATO) has played a crucial role in shaping the security architecture of Europe and beyond. Initially formed as a collective defense alliance to counter the threat of Soviet expansion during the Cold War, NATO has grown significantly over the decades. Its expansion, especially after the end of the Cold War, has been a source of both strategic opportunities and significant geopolitical tensions. The inclusion of Eastern European countries in NATO has been seen by many as a natural progression of the alliance's commitment to security and democracy, but it has also been viewed by Russia as a direct challenge to its sphere of influence and a provocative shift in the balance of power in Europe.

The expansion of NATO in the 1990s, following the collapse of the Soviet Union, was one of the most transformative and contentious periods in the alliance's history. Initially, the inclusion of former Warsaw Pact members like Poland, Hungary, and the Czech Republic seemed like an acknowledgment of their desire for security and alignment with the West after decades of Soviet control. For these countries, NATO membership was seen as a guarantee of protection from Russian influence and a step toward greater integration with the European Union. NATO's enlargement in the post-Soviet period symbolized the triumph of democracy and free-market capitalism over communism, with the alliance offering a security umbrella to countries seeking to distance themselves from Moscow's control.

However, the eastward expansion of NATO has been one of the most contentious issues in relations between Russia and the West. From the outset, Russia has viewed NATO's enlargement as a breach of assurances made by Western leaders at the time of German reunification in 1990, when it was suggested that NATO would not expand "one inch eastward." While no formal treaty was signed to codify these assurances, Russia has long felt that the expansion of NATO into former Soviet states and Eastern Europe represents a direct encroachment on its sphere of influence and national security. The inclusion of former Soviet republics such as the Baltic states

(Estonia, Latvia, and Lithuania) into NATO in 2004, followed by discussions of Ukraine and Georgia potentially joining the alliance, has only intensified Russia's sense of vulnerability.

The consequences of NATO's expansion have been profound, particularly for Russia, which has sought to retain its dominance in the post-Soviet space. For Russia, NATO enlargement represents a strategic threat, as it brings Western military influence closer to its borders, particularly in the Black Sea region and along its western frontier. The possibility of Ukraine and Georgia, both of which have had historically close ties to Russia, joining NATO has been viewed as an existential threat to Russian security. In response, Russia has employed various methods to prevent these countries from integrating into the alliance, including military intervention, covert operations, and political pressure. Russia's annexation of Crimea in 2014 and its military involvement in Eastern Ukraine are part of this broader effort to prevent NATO's further encroachment.

Beyond the immediate security concerns, NATO's expansion has also sparked a wider ideological and geopolitical struggle. The alliance's spread has been framed by Russia as a challenge to its political and cultural identity. Russia perceives NATO as an instrument of Western dominance, promoting liberal democratic values and market-driven economic systems that Russia sees as antithetical to its more authoritarian model. As a result, Putin's government has sought to establish alternatives to the West's liberal international order, both by asserting control over neighboring countries and by forging closer ties with other authoritarian regimes like China and Iran. The Russian leadership has actively promoted the idea of a multipolar world order, where Russia plays a central role in countering Western influence and shaping global governance.

NATO expansion has also had significant implications for European security and stability. While many of the new member states have benefited from the alliance's protection, NATO's presence in Eastern Europe has also created a sense of division between the West and Russia. The alliance's military deployments in Eastern Europe, particularly the deployment of NATO troops to countries like Poland, the Baltic States, and Romania, have been interpreted by Russia as a provocation. The stationing of U.S. missile defense systems in Eastern Europe has further heightened tensions, with Russia accusing the West of attempting to neutralize its nuclear deterrent and shift the strategic balance in Europe. In response, Russia has modernized its military forces and increased its military presence along its western border, conducting large-scale military exercises and improving its nuclear capabilities.

For NATO members, the expansion has reinforced their security but also presented challenges in terms of unity and strategy. The inclusion of new members, especially those with historical ties to Russia, has required NATO to balance its collective defense commitments with the need to avoid direct confrontation with Russia. The alliance's mission has evolved from countering the Soviet threat to addressing emerging security challenges, such as cyber threats, terrorism, and the instability caused by Russia's actions in Ukraine and Georgia. The ongoing tensions over NATO's role in Eastern Europe, particularly its relationship with Ukraine, have tested the alliance's cohesion and its ability to manage relations with Russia without provoking further conflict.

In conclusion, NATO expansion has reshaped the security landscape of Europe and has had significant repercussions for international relations. While it has provided security guarantees to former Soviet states and Eastern European nations, it has also deepened the divide between Russia and the West. NATO's growth has been seen by Russia as an existential threat, prompting military interventions and political resistance to further enlargement. The ongoing conflict in Ukraine and Russia's increasing efforts to challenge NATO's influence underscore the high stakes of this geopolitical struggle. As NATO continues to grapple with its expansion and its future direction, the repercussions of its post-Cold War growth will continue to shape global security dynamics for the foreseeable future.

Chapter 4
Cyber Warfare: A New Frontier

In the 21st century, the battlefield has expanded beyond traditional military theaters to include a new and increasingly influential domain: cyberspace. Cyber warfare has emerged as one of the most potent tools in modern geopolitics, offering state and non-state actors the ability to disrupt, deceive, and damage their adversaries without firing a single shot. Unlike conventional warfare, cyber attacks are often invisible, conducted in real-time, and can cause significant damage to infrastructure, economies, and political systems without direct military confrontation. For Russia, cyber warfare has become an integral part of its strategy to undermine its adversaries, particularly the West, by targeting the vulnerabilities in critical systems and sowing confusion and discord within societies.

Russia has been a pioneer in the use of cyber warfare as a strategic tool, exploiting the anonymity and global reach of the internet to conduct operations that can range from cyber espionage to full-blown cyber attacks. The Kremlin has used these capabilities to advance its geopolitical agenda, targeting governments, corporations, and institutions in both the United States and Europe. One of the most prominent examples of Russia's cyber aggression came during the 2016 U.S. presidential election, where Russian hackers conducted a series of attacks designed to influence public opinion, steal sensitive information, and sow distrust in the democratic process. These operations were not just aimed at tactical gains but were also part of a broader effort to destabilize Western democracies and challenge the liberal order that Russia perceives as a threat to its own political system.

Beyond elections, Russia's cyber operations have targeted critical infrastructure, including power grids, financial systems, and communication networks. These attacks are often designed to inflict economic damage, create political chaos, and weaken the cohesion of the adversary's internal systems. For Russia, cyber warfare is a low-cost, high-impact method of achieving its objectives without the risk of escalation that comes with traditional military engagements. This chapter explores the rise of cyber warfare as a new frontier in international relations, examining how Russia has harnessed this technology to challenge Western powers, destabilize regions, and reshape global geopolitics. It also looks at the challenges faced by governments and organizations in defending against these ever-evolving threats and the implications for the future of global security.

Russia's Cyber Capabilities and Tactics

Russia has developed one of the most sophisticated and effective cyber capabilities in the world, becoming a central player in the emerging landscape of cyber warfare. Over the past two decades, Russian cyber activities have evolved from initial cyber espionage to large-scale operations designed to disrupt political, economic, and military stability in adversarial states. These capabilities are not just the product of individual hackers or criminal groups, but are deeply integrated into Russia's broader national security strategy, supported by state-sponsored actors, military intelligence units, and private entities with close ties to the Kremlin. Russia's cyber operations reflect its focus on achieving strategic objectives while avoiding the risks and consequences of direct military confrontation.

One of the key components of Russia's cyber capabilities is its use of advanced hacking groups, most notably the cyber espionage and sabotage units linked to Russia's military intelligence agency, the GRU (Main Intelligence Directorate). These groups, such as APT28 (also known as Fancy Bear) and APT29 (Cozy Bear), are highly skilled at conducting operations that target government institutions, businesses, and infrastructure. These groups have been implicated in several high-profile cyberattacks, including the hacking of the Democratic National Committee (DNC) in the United States in 2016. The stolen emails were then leaked online, with the aim of influencing the U.S. presidential election. This operation, which was part of a broader disinformation campaign, was designed not only to steal sensitive information but to weaken trust in the democratic process and create division within the American political system.

Russia's cyber capabilities extend beyond espionage and data theft. The Kremlin has also invested heavily in developing disruptive cyber tactics that can cause physical damage to critical infrastructure. A prime example of this is the 2015 cyberattack on Ukraine's power grid, widely attributed to Russian state-sponsored hackers. The attack caused widespread blackouts, affecting over 200,000 people. This type of cyberattack demonstrates Russia's ability to conduct cyber warfare in the traditional sense of the term—targeting infrastructure and public services to create economic and political chaos. Similar tactics were employed in the 2017 NotPetya attack, which affected Ukraine but spread globally, causing billions of dollars in damage to multinational corporations and governments. While the primary target was Ukraine, the attack demonstrated Russia's ability to wield cyber tools as a form of economic sabotage and a means of destabilizing adversaries.

Another key tactic employed by Russian cyber units is the use of disinformation and influence operations, leveraging cyber tools to manipulate public opinion and disrupt democratic processes. Russian influence operations often involve creating fake social media accounts, spreading divisive narratives, and amplifying existing political tensions within target countries. The Internet Research Agency (IRA), a Russian troll farm with close ties to the Kremlin, is responsible for generating a significant amount of the disinformation campaigns. These campaigns have been aimed at influencing elections, exacerbating social divisions, and undermining trust in public institutions. The 2016 U.S. presidential election was one of the most notable examples, with Russian operatives using social media platforms like Facebook, Twitter, and Instagram to spread misleading information, promote fake news, and manipulate voter behavior. The IRA's tactics were designed to sow division, polarize the electorate, and create an environment of distrust and confusion. By exploiting societal divisions, Russia has been able to weaken its adversaries from within, without having to engage in direct conflict.

Beyond these tactics, Russia has also developed advanced cyber tools and technologies to target critical infrastructure and military systems of adversaries. In particular, the Russian government has cultivated a close relationship between its intelligence agencies and private technology firms, allowing for the development and use of sophisticated malware and ransomware that can evade detection and cause widespread disruption. Tools like the notorious malware "NotPetya" and "BadRabbit" are designed to cause chaos by encrypting data, disrupting operations, and demanding ransom payments. In some cases, these attacks have not only targeted government systems but also private businesses, financial institutions, and transportation networks, illustrating Russia's broader cyber strategy of attacking both public and private sectors to destabilize societies.

Russia's cyber tactics are also closely tied to its broader strategy of hybrid warfare, which combines conventional military actions with non-traditional forms of aggression, including cyber attacks. The cyber domain allows Russia to conduct operations at a fraction of the cost and risk of conventional warfare, while still achieving significant strategic goals. By targeting the information systems, power grids, and communications infrastructure of its adversaries, Russia is able to create confusion and undermine the coherence of the target's government and military operations. This type of hybrid warfare gives Russia a potent tool for influencing events in a way that is hard to attribute and difficult for adversaries to defend against.

Russia's cyber capabilities also highlight a new reality in the way global conflicts are waged. Cyber attacks can be launched anonymously, with the ability to scale up or down based on strategic goals. These attacks allow Russia to maintain plausible deniability, making it harder for adversaries to respond effectively or to hold the Kremlin accountable for the actions of its cyber units. The lack of clear rules governing state-sponsored cyber activities further complicates the global response to such actions. As cyber warfare continues to evolve, Russia's role as a leader in this field will likely shape future conflicts and the international norms that govern the use of cyber tools in statecraft.

In conclusion, Russia's cyber capabilities and tactics are central to its broader strategy of asserting influence, destabilizing adversaries, and challenging the global order without the need for traditional military conflict. The use of cyber espionage, disinformation, and infrastructure sabotage has allowed Russia to achieve its geopolitical goals in ways that are often difficult to trace or retaliate against. As the world becomes increasingly interconnected and dependent on digital technologies, Russia's growing expertise in cyber warfare will continue to pose a significant challenge to global security, requiring nations to rethink their defenses and responses to this new frontier of warfare.

The Role of Disinformation and Election Interference

In recent years, disinformation and election interference have emerged as critical tools of statecraft, particularly in the context of Russian cyber activities. Russia has become a global leader in the use of these tactics, leveraging both traditional media and the digital realm to manipulate public opinion, influence political outcomes, and destabilize democratic societies. Disinformation is the deliberate spread of false or misleading information, often designed to sow confusion, exacerbate societal divisions, and undermine trust in key institutions such as the government, media, and electoral systems. Election interference, on the other hand, involves attempts by external actors to disrupt the electoral process, manipulate voting behavior, or alter the outcome of elections, often through cyberattacks or by spreading false narratives.

Russia's interest in disinformation and election interference can be traced back to its broader geopolitical strategy of weakening its adversaries and challenging the liberal international order. The Kremlin has long viewed Western democracies—especially the United States and European Union—as ideological and strategic rivals. In particular, the expansion of liberal democratic ideals and Western institutions, such as NATO and the EU, is seen as a direct challenge to Russia's sovereignty and political model. By targeting the electoral systems of democratic nations, Russia seeks to destabilize these societies from within, creating divisions and undermining the public's confidence in their political systems. This strategy is an integral part of Russia's broader hybrid warfare doctrine, which combines traditional military force with non-traditional means, including cyberattacks and information operations, to achieve strategic objectives.

One of the most high-profile instances of Russian disinformation and election interference occurred during the 2016 U.S. presidential election. Russian intelligence agencies, particularly the GRU (Main Intelligence Directorate), conducted a wide-ranging campaign to influence the outcome of the election in favor of then-candidate Donald Trump. This operation included hacking into the Democratic National Committee (DNC) and the email accounts of senior campaign officials, stealing sensitive information, and leaking it online. The goal was to damage the Clinton campaign and create division within the American political system. Additionally, Russia deployed a network of social media bots and troll farms, such as the Internet Research Agency (IRA), to amplify divisive political messages, spread fake news, and exacerbate existing social tensions. By using social media platforms like Facebook, Twitter, and Instagram, Russian operatives targeted key demographic groups in swing states, spreading misleading narratives and false information about both candidates. This disinformation campaign was not only aimed at swaying voters but at creating confusion and distrust in the electoral process itself.

The Russian interference in the 2016 U.S. election was a wake-up call for many democracies, highlighting the vulnerabilities in the digital age and the ease with which foreign powers can influence the political landscape. Since then, Russia has continued to use disinformation and election interference as tools to challenge the

West, targeting elections in other countries, including France, Germany, and the United Kingdom. In some cases, these efforts have been more direct, such as in the form of hacking and leaking documents, while in others, Russia has focused on spreading divisive narratives and exploiting existing political and social divides within these countries. The Kremlin's disinformation operations have proven to be highly adaptive, evolving with the technological landscape and utilizing emerging platforms like messaging apps and alternative social media networks to bypass traditional media channels.

In addition to its election interference efforts, Russia has used disinformation to weaken trust in democratic institutions and undermine faith in the media. State-controlled Russian media outlets, such as RT and Sputnik, have played a significant role in spreading pro-Kremlin narratives while discrediting Western media outlets as biased or part of a larger "fake news" conspiracy. This tactic is designed to sow doubt and confusion, making it harder for citizens to discern truth from falsehood. In this way, Russia's disinformation strategy extends beyond elections and into the broader realm of public discourse, where it seeks to destabilize the social fabric of democracies by pitting citizens against one another and eroding the credibility of traditional institutions.

Russia's success in using disinformation and election interference is partly due to the growing polarization within many Western societies. As social media platforms have become the primary source of news for many people, they have also become fertile ground for disinformation campaigns. Echo chambers and filter bubbles, where individuals are exposed primarily to information that aligns with their pre-existing beliefs, have made it easier for disinformation to spread unchecked. The sheer volume of content on these platforms, combined with the speed at which information spreads, means that false narratives can go viral before they are debunked. This environment has made it difficult for governments, tech companies, and civil society organizations to effectively combat disinformation and its influence on democratic processes.

The consequences of these disinformation campaigns are far-reaching. Beyond the immediate impact of election interference, they contribute to a broader erosion of democratic values. By undermining public confidence in electoral outcomes, creating social division, and spreading false narratives, Russia's disinformation efforts seek to weaken the foundation of democratic societies. The result is a population that is increasingly polarized, distrustful of their institutions, and susceptible to manipulation by external actors. As the digital landscape continues to evolve, the threat posed by disinformation and election interference will only grow, making it critical for governments and societies to develop robust defenses against these tactics.

In conclusion, Russia's use of disinformation and election interference is a powerful tool in its broader strategy to challenge the West and weaken democratic societies. By exploiting vulnerabilities in electoral systems, media landscapes, and social divisions, Russia has been able to achieve its geopolitical objectives without resorting to direct military action. As the world becomes more interconnected and reliant on digital platforms, combating these threats will require coordinated efforts across governments, tech companies, and civil society to safeguard the integrity of elections and maintain trust in democratic institutions.

America's Vulnerabilities in the Digital Age

In the digital age, the United States, like many other nations, faces a new array of security challenges that were largely unseen in the pre-internet era. The rapid integration of digital technologies into every aspect of American life has created vast opportunities for innovation, communication, and economic growth. However, this interconnectedness has also exposed the country to significant vulnerabilities, particularly in the realms of cyber warfare, information security, and the integrity of its democratic processes. As a global leader in technology and digital infrastructure, the U.S. is both a target and a key player in the evolving battle for control over cyberspace.

One of the most significant vulnerabilities America faces in the digital age is the potential for cyberattacks on critical infrastructure. The country's reliance on digital technologies has made essential systems, such as power grids, water supply networks, and transportation systems, increasingly susceptible to cyber threats. Over the past decade, there have been numerous cyberattacks on U.S. infrastructure, ranging from ransomware attacks on healthcare systems to sophisticated hacking campaigns targeting energy grids. These attacks can have catastrophic consequences, not only causing economic disruptions but also endangering national security. Foreign adversaries, including Russia, China, and Iran, have been implicated in a variety of cyberattacks, often designed to sabotage or disrupt the nation's critical systems. The most notable example of this is the 2015 cyberattack on Ukraine's power grid, which experts have warned could be replicated in the U.S., highlighting the vulnerabilities in America's infrastructure and the potential consequences of a large-scale cyber assault.

In addition to infrastructure, another key vulnerability in the digital age is the growing threat of cyber espionage. As digital systems have become increasingly interconnected, they have also become prime targets for foreign intelligence agencies seeking to steal sensitive information. The U.S. government, military, and private sector are frequently targeted by hackers looking to gain access to confidential data, intellectual property, and national security secrets. High-profile breaches, such as the 2015 hack of the U.S. Office of Personnel Management (OPM), where the personal information of over 21 million federal employees was stolen, reveal just how exposed the country's digital systems are to espionage. China has been widely accused of carrying out extensive cyber espionage campaigns to gather intelligence on U.S. military technologies, government secrets, and economic data. The theft of intellectual property through cyber espionage also has profound economic implications, as it allows adversaries to bypass costly research and development processes and gain competitive advantages in technology markets.

Perhaps one of the most insidious vulnerabilities in the digital age is the manipulation of public opinion through disinformation campaigns. The U.S. has become a prime target for foreign actors who seek to influence political processes and destabilize social structures by exploiting the digital landscape. Russian interference in the 2016 U.S. presidential election serves as a stark reminder of the power of digital manipulation. Using social media platforms, Russian operatives spread disinformation, exacerbated social divisions, and even attempted to influence voting behavior through fake news, memes, and targeted ads. The use of social media to influence public opinion has only grown since then, with adversaries continuing to exploit the platforms' reach and algorithmic targeting to promote divisive narratives and sway elections. The digital space has democratized information dissemination, allowing anyone with an internet connection to reach millions, which has proven both beneficial and detrimental. This manipulation of information has led to a more polarized electorate, undermining trust in public institutions, and weakening the democratic process.

Moreover, the U.S. faces significant vulnerabilities in the realm of data privacy and surveillance. The massive amount of personal data collected through digital platforms, from social media to online shopping and healthcare records, presents both economic opportunities and serious risks. The collection and sale of personal data by tech companies, often without full transparency or consent, have raised concerns about privacy and security. The recent Facebook-Cambridge Analytica scandal, where data from millions of American users was harvested and used for political targeting, exposed the lack of regulation and oversight in data practices. Additionally, the ability of both foreign and domestic actors to exploit this data for nefarious purposes, including surveillance, identity theft, and manipulation, further exacerbates concerns about digital privacy. As digital systems evolve, so too do the tactics used by adversaries to gather, exploit, and weaponize personal information for strategic advantage.

Finally, the digital divide and reliance on technology have left large portions of the American population vulnerable to digital exclusion, misinformation, and cybercrime. Not all citizens have equal access to technology or the knowledge to navigate the complexities of the digital world safely. This digital inequality is particularly evident in marginalized communities, where access to high-speed internet and digital literacy programs is limited. The rise of online scams, phishing attacks, and financial fraud has disproportionately affected these populations, who are less likely to be aware of cybersecurity best practices. As the U.S. continues to embrace new digital technologies, ensuring equitable access to technology and education becomes an increasingly important factor in mitigating the risks associated with the digital age.

In conclusion, America's vulnerabilities in the digital age are far-reaching and multifaceted. From cyberattacks on critical infrastructure to the exploitation of personal data, foreign interference in elections, and the spread of disinformation, the U.S. faces new and evolving threats in cyberspace. As digital systems become more deeply integrated into every aspect of American life, addressing these vulnerabilities will require a coordinated effort across government, industry, and civil society to strengthen cybersecurity defenses, ensure transparency in data practices, and safeguard the integrity of democratic processes. The digital age offers immense opportunities, but it also presents significant challenges that must be met with vigilance and proactive strategies to protect the nation's security and values.

Chapter 5
Undermining Democracy

In an era of increasing global interconnectedness, the core principles of democracy—freedom of speech, the rule of law, and the right to free and fair elections—have become vulnerable to manipulation and subversion. Russia, under Vladimir Putin's leadership, has become one of the most active and strategic actors in attempting to undermine democratic systems, particularly in Western nations. While Russia's government continues to tout its commitment to sovereignty and national pride, its actions in cyberspace, media manipulation, and political interference have sought to destabilize democratic institutions, weaken public trust in governments, and create divisions within societies. These tactics, often covert and insidious, represent a significant shift in the methods used to achieve geopolitical objectives without engaging in traditional forms of warfare.

At the heart of Russia's strategy to undermine democracy is the use of disinformation campaigns and the manipulation of information. Russian operatives, both state-sponsored and aligned with the Kremlin, have used digital platforms and traditional media to spread false narratives, sow discord, and influence public opinion. The 2016 U.S. presidential election serves as a high-profile example of how Russia employed social media disinformation, hacking, and leaking techniques to sway voter behavior and erode faith in the electoral process. This strategy goes beyond just influencing specific political outcomes; it aims to create confusion and undermine the legitimacy of democratic systems themselves. By amplifying divisions within society—whether ideological, racial, or political—Russia seeks to destabilize the very fabric of democratic societies, eroding their cohesion and threatening their ability to function effectively.

In addition to disinformation, Russia has also employed more direct methods of influence, such as supporting extremist political movements, fostering corruption, and exploiting vulnerabilities in political systems. The Kremlin has been known to provide support, whether financial or logistical, to far-right and far-left parties in Europe, hoping to weaken the influence of centrist, pro-European political forces. This creates an environment of political instability where extreme factions gain more visibility and power, often through populist rhetoric that challenges the status quo. Through these efforts, Russia has not only targeted individual countries but has also sought to weaken the European Union and NATO, both of which represent the collective values and institutions that Russia sees as opposing its own autocratic model. This chapter explores how these various tactics of undermining democracy—through disinformation, political manipulation, and support for extremist movements—fit into Russia's broader strategic objective of destabilizing the West and limiting the influence of liberal democracies.

Putin's Support for Anti-Democratic Movements

Vladimir Putin's Russia has strategically supported anti-democratic movements across the globe as part of its broader geopolitical and ideological objectives. Under Putin's leadership, Russia has increasingly aligned itself with authoritarian regimes and political movements that challenge liberal democratic norms. This support is rooted in Russia's desire to weaken Western influence, particularly in Europe and North America, while promoting its own vision of governance, which prioritizes state control, nationalism, and traditional values over democratic principles. Through a combination of diplomatic, financial, and sometimes military support, Putin's Russia has sought to foster instability in countries that promote liberal democracy, positioning itself as a champion of sovereign nations that reject Western-led globalism.

One of the most notable examples of Putin's support for anti-democratic movements has been his backing of far-right, populist, and nationalist political parties in Europe. These movements, often characterized by their anti-immigrant, anti-European Union (EU), and anti-globalization stances, align with Russia's desire to disrupt the European project and weaken the unity of Western alliances. Putin has cultivated relationships with key figures and political parties in countries such as France, Hungary, Austria, and Italy, offering them moral, political, and sometimes financial support. For example, Marine Le Pen's National Rally in France has received financial support from Russian banks, and Le Pen herself has met with Putin on several occasions, expressing admiration for his strongman leadership style. Similarly, Viktor Orbán, the Prime Minister of Hungary, has pursued an increasingly authoritarian agenda, undermining democratic institutions within Hungary while fostering close ties with Moscow. Orbán's government has rejected EU pressure to uphold democratic norms, embracing Russia's model of governance as an alternative.

In addition to supporting far-right movements in Europe, Putin has also aligned himself with authoritarian leaders in countries such as Syria, Venezuela, and Belarus. These regimes share a common interest in resisting Western influence and the spread of liberal democratic values. Putin has provided both direct and indirect support to these regimes, offering political backing, military assistance, and economic aid. In Syria, Russia's military intervention on behalf of Bashar al-Assad helped stabilize his government, which had been facing a popular uprising and subsequent civil war. Russia's support for Assad has been framed as part of its broader strategy to retain influence in the Middle East, but it also reflects Putin's commitment to supporting fellow autocrats who resist democratization and Western-style governance. Similarly, in Venezuela, Russia has provided economic and military support to Nicolás Maduro's regime, which has been accused of widespread corruption, human rights abuses, and the suppression of political opposition. By propping up these regimes, Russia seeks to challenge the global norms of democracy and human rights while ensuring that its influence remains strong in regions critical to its strategic interests.

Putin's support for anti-democratic movements extends to Russia's broader efforts to weaken democratic institutions within its neighboring countries, particularly in the post-Soviet space. Russia's annexation of Crimea in 2014 and its involvement in the ongoing conflict in eastern Ukraine were not only about territorial expansion but also about destabilizing the region and preventing Ukraine from integrating with Western institutions like NATO and the EU. Russia has consistently worked to sow discord within Ukraine, supporting pro-Russian separatist movements and promoting political factions that favor closer ties with Russia. This strategy aims to prevent the spread of democratic values and pro-Western ideologies in countries that were once part of the Soviet Union, preserving Russia's influence over its neighbors and counteracting the encroachment of Western powers in the region.

In addition to direct political support, Russia has used its control over media outlets to promote anti-democratic ideologies both domestically and abroad. State-controlled Russian media outlets such as RT (Russia Today) and Sputnik have played a significant role in spreading disinformation, undermining trust in democratic institutions, and promoting narratives that favor authoritarian governance. These media outlets have been used to target Western democracies, particularly during elections, by disseminating divisive messages, spreading fake news, and amplifying extremist views. By engaging in these activities, Russia not only promotes its own political agenda but also seeks to destabilize the political climates of democratic countries and reduce the credibility of liberal democratic institutions.

Russia's support for anti-democratic movements is also driven by its ideological opposition to Western liberalism, which it views as a threat to its sovereignty and values. Putin has positioned himself as the leader of a global movement that resists what he perceives as Western attempts to impose liberal democracy, human rights, and free-market capitalism on the rest of the world. In this context, Putin's support for anti-democratic forces can be seen as part of a broader strategy to create a counterweight to the West and defend a world order that is more aligned with Russia's authoritarian political model. By supporting anti-democratic movements and leaders, Putin hopes to reshape the global balance of power and limit the influence of the United States and its European allies.

In conclusion, Putin's support for anti-democratic movements is a key aspect of his broader strategy to challenge the liberal international order and promote an alternative model of governance that emphasizes nationalism, state control, and centralized power. Through financial, political, and military support, as well as the use of media to spread disinformation, Russia has worked to foster instability in democratic societies and support authoritarian regimes that resist Western influence. Whether in Europe, the Middle East, or Latin America, Putin's actions reflect his belief that the future of global governance should not be dictated by liberal democratic principles but rather by a multipolar world order where authoritarian regimes can thrive.

The Weaponization of Corruption

The weaponization of corruption has become a powerful tool in Russia's foreign policy, serving as a means to exert influence, destabilize governments, and advance its geopolitical interests without resorting to traditional military force. Corruption, when strategically deployed by state actors, can undermine political systems, disrupt economies, and erode the legitimacy of democratic institutions. Russia has skillfully utilized this tactic as part of its broader strategy to weaken its adversaries, particularly in Europe, the United States, and former Soviet republics. By fostering corruption within key political, economic, and financial systems, Russia has been able to create instability, manipulate political processes, and extend its influence across the globe, all while maintaining plausible deniability.

The first element of the weaponization of corruption lies in Russia's support for kleptocratic regimes and corrupt political elites. Putin's government has cultivated relationships with authoritarian leaders who engage in corrupt practices, using them as instruments to secure Russia's interests in their countries. In many cases, these regimes are economically dependent on Russia and are willing to turn a blind eye to corruption, often as part of an unspoken arrangement where Russia provides political, economic, or military support in exchange for access to resources, strategic positioning, or political loyalty. This mutual benefit reinforces the status quo and allows

Russia to maintain influence over countries that would otherwise seek alignment with the West.

A prime example of this strategy is Russia's close relationship with the leadership in Central Asia, particularly in countries like Kazakhstan, Uzbekistan, and Turkmenistan. These nations, while nominally independent, have struggled with endemic corruption, and Russia has exploited this weakness to maintain its foothold in the region. By supporting corrupt leaders and offering them economic or military assistance, Russia has ensured that these governments remain aligned with Moscow rather than seeking closer ties with Western powers or regional institutions like NATO or the European Union. In return, Russia has secured favorable trade agreements, access to energy resources, and strategic military partnerships. This corrupt alliance prevents these countries from pursuing independent or pro-Western foreign policies, thus extending Russia's sphere of influence.

Russia has also used corruption as a tool to destabilize neighboring countries, particularly those in Eastern Europe and the former Soviet space. One of the most prominent examples is Ukraine, where corruption has long been a major challenge. Russia has actively fostered corrupt practices within Ukraine's political and business elite, using these ties to manipulate Ukraine's internal affairs. The relationship between the Kremlin and oligarchs in Ukraine has been crucial in Russia's efforts to influence political decisions, destabilize the country, and prevent Ukraine from moving closer to the European Union and NATO. By fostering corruption at the highest levels, Russia has been able to weaken Ukraine's ability to implement reforms, curb Russian influence, and pursue greater integration with Western institutions.

In the case of European democracies, Russia has sought to exploit corruption as a way to create divisions and undermine trust in political systems. The Russian government has been linked to a number of corrupt practices that have been aimed at influencing elections, political decisions, and the behavior of key leaders in Europe. Russian oligarchs and businesses have made investments in European companies, particularly in sectors like energy, media, and real estate, using these financial ties to gain leverage over European politicians and institutions. By channeling money through corrupt networks, Russia has been able to secure favorable policies and weaken opposition to its geopolitical objectives. In this way, corruption has served as a form of "soft power," enabling Russia to manipulate domestic politics and foster divisions within the European Union and NATO.

The weaponization of corruption also extends to Russia's use of money laundering, which has become a key mechanism for undermining global financial systems and promoting instability. Russian oligarchs and government officials have used various methods to move illicit funds through international financial institutions, ensuring that money is shielded from scrutiny. This illegal flow of capital has allowed corrupt leaders to enrich themselves at the expense of their countries, while also providing Russia with a way to exert economic influence over foreign governments. The London property market, for example, has become a major destination for illicit Russian money, with politicians and oligarchs using the city's luxury real estate market to launder funds and gain access to influential circles. By creating complex webs of financial transactions that are difficult to trace, Russia has been able to create a financial infrastructure that is resistant to Western sanctions and scrutiny, further cementing its ability to destabilize regions and exert influence over foreign governments.

In addition to directly supporting corrupt regimes and individuals, Russia has used the spread of corruption to create an environment of political paralysis and inefficiency in target countries. The corrosive effect of corruption is profound: it erodes trust in public institutions, leads to the misallocation of resources, and stifles economic development. In countries where corruption is widespread, citizens lose faith in their leaders, creating an opening for political instability and social unrest. By fostering corruption, Russia has been able to exploit these vulnerabilities, often pushing nations into a cycle of political gridlock that prevents meaningful reform and weakens their capacity to resist foreign influence.

The weaponization of corruption also has a significant impact on the international rules-based order. Corruption undermines transparency, accountability, and the rule of law—core principles upon which democratic systems and international relations are built. By promoting corruption, Russia contributes to the erosion of these values, making it more difficult for global institutions like the United Nations, the World Bank, and the International Monetary Fund to function effectively. The persistence of corruption weakens the legitimacy of international agreements, destabilizes markets, and encourages the proliferation of authoritarianism, all of which work against the broader goals of peace, security, and democratic governance.

In conclusion, Russia's use of corruption as a tool of foreign policy is a critical component of its strategy to destabilize adversaries, extend its global influence, and promote a world order that is favorable to its interests. By supporting corrupt regimes, fostering illicit financial networks, and exploiting weaknesses in democratic institutions, Russia has effectively weaponized corruption to undermine Western democracies, expand its influence in neighboring regions, and challenge the global liberal order. This approach represents a new form of warfare, one that is difficult to combat with traditional military responses, requiring innovative strategies to counteract the corrosive effects of corruption on both national and global levels.

Exploiting Divisions Within the West

Russia, under the leadership of Vladimir Putin, has made a strategic and consistent effort to exploit divisions within Western democracies, seeking to undermine their cohesion and weaken the alliances that define the liberal international order. The Kremlin views the unity of Western powers—particularly the United States, the European Union (EU), and NATO—as a major threat to its geopolitical goals. As such, Russia has employed a variety of tactics, ranging from disinformation and cyberattacks to fostering political instability, with the ultimate aim of sowing discord and diminishing the West's collective influence. By capitalizing on existing political, social, and economic fractures within Western societies, Russia has been able to weaken the Western alliance and challenge its global leadership.

One of the most effective tools Russia has used to exploit divisions within the West is disinformation. Through state-sponsored media outlets such as RT (Russia Today) and Sputnik, Russia has spread false narratives, conspiracy theories, and divisive content to target political and social vulnerabilities in democratic societies. These media outlets, while presenting themselves as independent news sources, are in fact heavily controlled by the Russian government and operate with the intent of distorting public perception and creating confusion. During major political events, such as elections in the United States, the United Kingdom, and France, Russia has actively engaged in campaigns to manipulate public opinion and amplify existing social divisions. In the 2016 U.S. presidential election, for example, Russian operatives utilized social media platforms to spread fake news, exploit racial and political tensions, and promote extremist views. By capitalizing on divisive issues—such as immigration, race relations, and nationalism—Russia was able to exacerbate existing fractures within American society, contributing to an atmosphere of distrust and polarization.

In addition to media manipulation, Russia has also employed cyberattacks and digital influence operations to undermine the integrity of democratic processes and destabilize Western governments. These cyber operations have been designed to target the electoral process directly, as well as to cause broader disruptions within key political and economic institutions. Russia's involvement in the hacking of the Democratic National Committee (DNC) during the 2016 U.S. election is one of the most well-documented examples of this tactic. By stealing sensitive information and leaking it to the public, Russia sought to damage the credibility of Hillary Clinton's campaign and create chaos within the Democratic Party. Similar attacks have targeted political institutions in other countries, including France, Germany, and the Netherlands, with the goal of weakening democratic structures and promoting pro-Russian candidates or policies.

Another significant aspect of Russia's strategy to exploit divisions within the West is its support for far-right, populist movements. These political movements, which often espouse nationalist, anti-immigrant, and anti-establishment rhetoric, are seen by Russia as potential allies in its broader effort to weaken the European Union and NATO. By supporting far-right political parties in countries like France, Germany, Hungary, and Italy, Russia has sought to amplify the voices of those who advocate for policies that are aligned with its interests. Russian state-controlled media has often provided favorable coverage to populist leaders, such as Marine Le Pen in France, Viktor Orbán in Hungary, and Matteo Salvini in Italy, offering them political legitimacy and, in some cases, financial support. These populist movements often share a common opposition to the EU and its policies, particularly in the areas of immigration and integration, making them fertile ground for Russian influence. By supporting these movements, Russia hopes to create division within the EU and erode the unity of NATO, undermining Western efforts to counter Russian aggression.

Russia's exploitation of Western divisions is not limited to electoral interference and media manipulation. The Kremlin has also sought to capitalize on economic and social tensions, particularly those driven by globalization, immigration, and economic inequality. In many Western countries, these issues have fueled populist movements and social unrest, creating an environment where division and distrust are prevalent. Russia has sought to exacerbate these tensions by promoting anti-globalization and anti-establishment narratives, which resonate with large segments of the population that feel alienated from mainstream political parties. By exploiting these economic and social divides, Russia has contributed to the rise of political movements that reject traditional institutions and the global order in favor of nationalism and isolationism.

The refugee crisis and immigration policies have also been focal points for Russian interference. By promoting anti-immigrant sentiment and amplifying fears about the erosion of national identity,

Russia has sought to exploit cultural divisions in European countries. For example, Russia-backed disinformation campaigns have spread false and inflammatory narratives about refugees and migrants, portraying them as a threat to national security and cultural values. This has fueled political polarization in several European countries, particularly in Germany, where the influx of refugees has sparked heated debates about immigration policy. By stoking these fears, Russia not only weakens public trust in political leaders but also fosters political polarization that makes it more difficult for governments to reach consensus on critical issues.

In conclusion, Russia's strategy to exploit divisions within the West is multifaceted and deeply rooted in its broader geopolitical goals. By using disinformation, cyberattacks, support for far-right movements, and the exacerbation of economic and social tensions, Russia has sought to weaken the cohesion of Western democracies and reduce their ability to act collectively. The Kremlin's actions aim not only to destabilize individual countries but also to challenge the liberal international order that underpins the unity of NATO, the European Union, and other Western institutions. As the digital landscape continues to evolve, so too will the methods used by Russia and other actors to exploit divisions within the West, making it crucial for Western countries to develop robust strategies to counter these tactics and preserve democratic values and unity.

Chapter 6
The Middle East: A Changing Landscape

The Middle East has long been a region marked by complex geopolitics, historical conflicts, and shifting alliances, and in recent years, it has experienced profound transformations that have redefined the strategic landscape. With the decline of traditional powers like the United States and the rise of new regional actors such as Russia and China, the Middle East is witnessing a power shift that is reshaping the global order. The region's importance remains undiminished, primarily due to its vast energy resources, strategic location at the crossroads of Europe, Asia, and Africa, and the ongoing conflicts that continue to draw in global powers. As the West's influence wanes, Russia has stepped in to fill the vacuum, using a combination of military intervention, political alliances, and economic partnerships to extend its influence and challenge the liberal international order.

Russia's involvement in the Middle East is not a new phenomenon, but its resurgence in recent years, particularly through its military intervention in Syria, has been a game-changer. By supporting the regime of Bashar al-Assad, Russia has solidified its position as a key player in the region, countering Western influence and asserting itself as a stabilizing force in countries beset by conflict. Russia's role in Syria, along with its growing ties to Iran, Hezbollah, and other regional players, has allowed it to build a network of alliances that are not only aimed at securing Russia's strategic interests but also at challenging the United States and its allies. This intervention has redefined the balance of power, making Russia an indispensable player in the Middle East's political and military dynamics.

At the same time, the Middle East's shifting landscape is shaped by the complex interplay of local conflicts, ideological rivalries, and the growing influence of non-state actors. From the ongoing wars in Yemen and Libya to the deepening rivalry between Sunni and Shia powers, the region remains embroiled in instability. New alliances are emerging, and old ones are being tested, with countries like Saudi Arabia, Turkey, and Israel recalibrating their foreign policies in response to changing geopolitical realities. The influence of external powers, particularly Russia and China, adds another layer of complexity, as these nations seek to enhance their presence and challenge traditional Western dominance. This chapter explores how the Middle East's evolving dynamics are reshaping the global order and examines the role of Russia as a central actor in this new geopolitical era.

Russia's Engagement in Syria

Russia's engagement in Syria represents a pivotal moment in its strategy to reassert itself as a global power and challenge Western influence in the Middle East. The Syrian conflict, which began in 2011 as part of the wider Arab Spring uprisings, quickly escalated into a multifaceted civil war involving numerous domestic and foreign actors. While the U.S. and European nations supported various opposition groups, seeking to oust President Bashar al-Assad, Russia took a staunch position in support of the Assad regime, both politically and militarily. Russia's involvement in Syria has had profound implications for the regional balance of power and has also marked a major turning point in Russian foreign policy, signaling its willingness to challenge the West directly and invest heavily in the Middle East.

Russia's intervention in Syria began in earnest in September 2015, when it launched an air campaign to support Assad's forces against the growing insurgency. This military intervention was driven by several key factors, most notably Russia's desire to maintain its influence in the region and prevent the collapse of the Syrian government, which was a critical ally for Moscow. Syria, under Assad, has been a long-time partner of Russia, hosting Russia's only naval base in the Mediterranean at Tartus and serving as a conduit for Russian arms sales to the region. Losing Syria to a Western-backed opposition would not only diminish Russia's influence in the Middle East but would also deprive it of a crucial strategic foothold. Additionally, Moscow viewed the Syrian conflict as an opportunity to weaken the influence of the United States and its allies in the region by preventing the fall of a key ally and challenging the legitimacy of Western interventionism.

In addition to political and strategic considerations, Russia's engagement in Syria was framed as part of its broader anti-terrorism stance, particularly against Islamist extremism. Russia portrayed its intervention as a necessary step to combat ISIS and other jihadist groups that were destabilizing Syria and Iraq. While Russia did indeed target ISIS and other radical groups, it is important to note that the majority of Russian airstrikes were aimed at Syrian opposition groups that posed a direct threat to Assad's regime rather than focusing exclusively on ISIS. This selective targeting, combined with Russia's ongoing military support for Assad's forces, reflected

Moscow's ultimate objective of ensuring the survival of the Assad regime and maintaining its strategic interests in Syria.

Russia's military involvement in Syria has involved a combination of air power, ground forces, and strategic support for Assad's military. The Russian Air Force has conducted thousands of airstrikes, using advanced weaponry to target rebel-held areas and infrastructure. These air campaigns, while effective in supporting the Syrian government's efforts to recapture territory, have also drawn widespread criticism for indiscriminately targeting civilian areas and contributing to the humanitarian crisis in the country. In addition to airstrikes, Russia has provided Assad with critical ground support, including military advisors, special forces, and advanced weaponry, bolstering the regime's ability to retake key regions from opposition forces. Russian forces have also established military bases in Syria, which serve as vital command centers for operations in the region and as a foothold for further influence in the Middle East.

One of the most significant aspects of Russia's engagement in Syria is its ability to leverage its military presence to forge stronger relationships with regional actors such as Iran, Hezbollah, and Turkey. Iran has been a key ally of Assad, providing military support and personnel, and Moscow has sought to maintain strong ties with Tehran to consolidate its influence in the region. The Russia-Iran partnership has created a powerful axis in Syria, where both countries work together to support Assad and counterbalance Western and regional opposition. Additionally, Russia's role as a mediator between Iran and Turkey, two countries with often opposing interests in Syria, has allowed Moscow to position itself as a critical player in any future peace negotiations.

Turkey, a NATO member and regional power with its own interests in Syria, has had a complicated relationship with Russia in the context of the Syrian conflict. Initially, Turkey opposed Assad's rule and backed Syrian opposition forces. However, as the conflict progressed, Turkey's priorities shifted, especially with regard to Kurdish groups operating in Syria, which Turkey views as a threat to its own security. Russia has been able to exploit this divergence by working with Turkey to facilitate joint military operations, such as in Idlib, Syria's last opposition stronghold, and promoting diplomatic discussions aimed at de-escalating tensions between Turkey and the Kurdish groups. Moscow's ability to broker agreements between these two rival powers has allowed it to increase its diplomatic leverage in Syria and solidify its role as a key power broker in the region.

On the global stage, Russia's engagement in Syria has also served as a counterpoint to U.S. influence in the Middle East. By intervening directly in the Syrian conflict, Russia has challenged U.S. leadership in the region and asserted its own power, particularly in the face of American-led coalition efforts to combat ISIS. Moscow has also used its position in Syria to question the legitimacy of Western interventions, often citing the absence of U.N. Security Council authorization for the U.S. and its allies' actions in Syria. By positioning itself as a defender of international law and the sovereignty of states, Russia has been able to appeal to other nations critical of Western interventions and use Syria as a platform to challenge the existing global order.

In conclusion, Russia's engagement in Syria is a critical component of its broader geopolitical strategy in the Middle East and beyond. The intervention has allowed Russia to maintain a significant influence in a region traditionally dominated by Western powers and to solidify its status as a key player in global geopolitics. Through military support for the Assad regime, strategic alliances with Iran and Hezbollah, and its ability to broker agreements between regional powers like Turkey, Russia has demonstrated its capacity to shape the outcome of conflicts and advance its strategic interests. Despite the considerable human and financial costs of the intervention, Russia's involvement in Syria has been successful in securing its position as a major player in Middle Eastern politics and challenging the influence of the United States and its allies in the region.

Aligning with Iran: A Strategic Partnership

Russia's alignment with Iran has evolved into one of the most significant geopolitical partnerships in the Middle East, marked by shared interests in countering U.S. influence, opposing Western-led international initiatives, and securing regional dominance. While Russia and Iran have historically had different ideological and strategic goals, their cooperation in recent years, particularly in Syria, has highlighted how pragmatic alliances can be forged in a region where national interests often take precedence over ideological affinity. The strategic partnership between Moscow and Tehran is built on mutual benefits, which include military cooperation, economic exchange, and the consolidation of influence in the Middle East.

One of the primary drivers of the Russia-Iran relationship is both nations' desire to challenge U.S. hegemony in the region. For Russia, Iran represents a valuable ally in its broader effort to counterbalance Western influence in the Middle East. Since the end of the Cold War, the United States has maintained a dominant military and diplomatic presence in the region, with key allies such as Saudi Arabia, Israel, and Turkey. Russia, keen on reasserting its global power, views Iran as an important partner in challenging this dominance, particularly in the wake of Russia's annexation of Crimea and its involvement in the conflict in Ukraine. Moscow has sought to create a coalition of countries that oppose U.S. policies, and Iran, with its long-standing antagonism toward the West, fits well within this framework.

The Syria conflict has served as the cornerstone of the Russia-Iran partnership. When the Syrian Civil War broke out in 2011, both Russia and Iran quickly recognized the strategic importance of maintaining the Assad regime in power. For Russia, Syria is a critical ally in the Middle East, offering the Russian navy access to its Mediterranean port at Tartus, which is Russia's only naval base in the region. Moscow also saw Syria as a key to its broader efforts to assert influence in the Middle East and to counter Western-backed opposition movements. For Iran, Syria has long been a critical ally in maintaining the "Resistance Axis," a network of Shia-aligned states and groups spanning from Tehran to Beirut, which includes Hezbollah in Lebanon and Iraqi Shia militias. Syria, under Assad, provided a vital supply line to Hezbollah, Iran's primary proxy in the region, and allowed Iran to project power throughout the Levant.

With both nations' interests aligning, Russia and Iran became crucial military partners in Syria, providing military assistance and strategic advice to Assad's forces. Russia's air power and advanced weaponry complemented Iran's ground support, which included supplying arms, training, and deploying Revolutionary Guard forces to fight alongside Assad's military. Russian airstrikes have focused on rebel-held areas, particularly those where Western-backed opposition groups operated, while Iranian forces and their allies have supported ground operations aimed at securing key regions. The coordination between the two countries has been instrumental in keeping Assad in power and has dramatically altered the course of the war. This partnership not only secured both countries' interests in Syria but also provided a direct challenge to U.S. and European-backed opposition forces.

Beyond Syria, the Russia-Iran alliance is also focused on economic cooperation, particularly in the energy sector. Both countries are major players in global energy markets, and their collaboration has allowed them to challenge the U.S.-dominated energy system. Russia, as one of the world's largest producers of natural gas and oil, has helped Iran evade Western sanctions, particularly after the U.S. withdrew from the 2015 Iran nuclear deal in 2018. Russia has provided Iran with critical technology and expertise in energy development, including help with oil and gas infrastructure, while also purchasing Iranian oil and natural gas. This economic exchange has allowed Iran to maintain its energy exports and bolster its economy, despite facing crippling sanctions. Conversely, Russia benefits from Iran's energy reserves and its strategic position as an energy hub in the Middle East.

The partnership between Russia and Iran also serves to undermine the existing security architecture in the Middle East, particularly the relationships between the United States and its allies in the region. Iran's support for militant groups such as Hezbollah in Lebanon and various Shiite militias in Iraq has long been a thorn in the side of U.S. and Israeli interests. By aligning with Iran, Russia has positioned itself as a counterbalance to American and Israeli influence in the region. Russia has also been able to capitalize on Iran's dissatisfaction with U.S. sanctions and its desire to create alliances that bypass Western-imposed restrictions. This alignment provides both countries with a strategic advantage by allowing them to exert influence over key regional conflicts and prevent the U.S. from maintaining full control over the Middle East's geopolitical landscape.

At the same time, Russia and Iran have maintained their respective independent interests, which sometimes complicate their cooperation. While both countries share a common adversary in the United States, their broader geopolitical goals sometimes diverge. For example, Russia has cultivated ties with other regional powers, including Israel, Turkey, and Saudi Arabia, which have conflicting interests with Iran. Russia has also been careful not to fully align with Iran on all regional issues, particularly in relation to Iran's nuclear ambitions, which remain a point of tension with both the West and some of its Middle Eastern allies. However, the pragmatic nature of their relationship has allowed both countries to navigate these complexities and maintain a functional partnership.

In conclusion, Russia's strategic alignment with Iran in the Middle East is a calculated move designed to enhance its regional influence, challenge U.S. power, and secure vital geopolitical and economic interests. By supporting Iran's military and economic goals in Syria and beyond, Russia has gained a valuable ally in its efforts to reshape the Middle Eastern order. The partnership between these two nations, while pragmatic and at times opportunistic, has significantly impacted the region, with Russia leveraging its relationship with Iran to challenge Western influence and assert its own power in the Middle East.

The Decline of America's Influence in the Region

The Middle East has traditionally been a region of critical importance to U.S. foreign policy, driven by its strategic location, energy resources, and longstanding political, economic, and military ties. However, in recent years, America's influence in the region has experienced a marked decline. This shift has been influenced by a combination of factors, including changing U.S. foreign policy priorities, regional power dynamics, and the growing influence of rival powers such as Russia and China. The decline of U.S. influence in the Middle East marks a significant departure from the post-Cold War era when the U.S. was the dominant global actor shaping events in the region.

One of the most significant factors contributing to the decline of American influence is the shifting focus of U.S. foreign policy. Over the past two decades, the U.S. has been deeply involved in the wars in Iraq and Afghanistan, leading to a heavy military and financial commitment that has strained resources and eroded public support for interventionist policies in the region. The Iraq War, in particular, has had long-lasting consequences. The 2003 invasion, ostensibly aimed at dismantling Saddam Hussein's regime and eliminating weapons of mass destruction, led to a protracted conflict that destabilized the entire region. The aftermath of the war saw the rise of sectarian violence, the emergence of ISIS, and the loss of American credibility in the region. The costly and unsuccessful military interventions in Iraq and Afghanistan have led many to question the effectiveness of American engagement in the Middle East and to prioritize domestic concerns over foreign entanglements.

Additionally, the Obama administration's "pivot to Asia" and its desire to reduce military commitments in the Middle East in favor of focusing on the Asia-Pacific region further contributed to the perception of a declining U.S. presence in the region. The U.S. sought to recalibrate its foreign policy, seeking to focus on emerging threats from China and Russia, and pivoting away from Middle Eastern conflicts that were seen as costly and difficult to resolve. This shift left a power vacuum in the region that was quickly filled by regional powers and external actors, particularly Russia and Iran.

Russia, under Vladimir Putin, has been one of the most prominent beneficiaries of the U.S. retreat from the Middle East. Russia's military intervention in Syria in 2015 marked its return to the region as a key player, decisively shifting the balance of power in favor of the Assad regime and challenging Western-led efforts to depose him. Moscow's support for the Syrian government, coupled with its alliances with Iran and Hezbollah, allowed Russia to become the dominant power broker in the Syrian conflict. Russia has also cultivated strong ties with other regional powers, including Turkey and Egypt, further cementing its position as a major geopolitical player in the Middle East. Russia's willingness to engage in direct military action, its support for authoritarian regimes, and its ability to broker deals with a range of actors, from Iran to Israel, has made it an influential force in shaping regional outcomes.

China has also expanded its influence in the Middle East, particularly through its Belt and Road Initiative (BRI), which seeks to improve infrastructure and foster economic ties across Asia, Africa, and Europe. The Middle East, as a key crossroads of global trade, is a critical part of China's economic vision. Beijing has invested heavily in the region, offering loans, investments, and infrastructure development in exchange for access to energy resources and strategic partnerships. China's growing economic presence in the region, coupled with its ability to offer an alternative to Western-style democratic governance, has made it an attractive partner for several Middle Eastern countries, including Saudi Arabia, the United Arab Emirates (UAE), and Iran. The U.S. has found itself increasingly sidelined as China offers a different approach, focusing on economic cooperation rather than military intervention and political conditionality.

The U.S. withdrawal from the Joint Comprehensive Plan of Action (JCPOA) with Iran in 2018, under President Donald Trump, also contributed to the decline of American influence in the region. The decision to unilaterally pull out of the nuclear deal not only strained relations with key European allies but also led to further instability in the region. The reimposition of sanctions on Iran escalated tensions, particularly with Tehran's increasing defiance and its support for proxy forces across the Middle East. The U.S.'s decision to abandon diplomatic efforts in favor of maximum pressure has led to a resurgence of Iran's influence in countries like Iraq, Syria, Lebanon, and Yemen, where it continues to challenge U.S. allies and interests.

Furthermore, the ongoing conflicts and instability in the region have made it increasingly difficult for the U.S. to maintain a coherent policy that balances competing interests. The Saudi-led war in Yemen, the ongoing Israeli-Palestinian conflict, and the fractured political situations in countries like Libya and Lebanon have created a web of challenges that the U.S. has struggled to address effectively. While the U.S. has maintained strong relationships with key regional allies such as Israel and Saudi Arabia, these partnerships have become increasingly strained over differing priorities and regional policies, particularly regarding Iran, human rights, and the role of non-state actors like Hezbollah and the Houthis.

In conclusion, the decline of America's influence in the Middle East is the result of a combination of factors, including overextension in military conflicts, the shifting focus of U.S. foreign policy, and the rising influence of adversaries like Russia and China. While the U.S.

remains a critical player in the region, its ability to shape outcomes and maintain dominant influence has been significantly challenged. As the Middle East becomes an increasingly multipolar region, the U.S. faces the challenge of recalibrating its role and navigating a complex landscape of shifting alliances, regional rivalries, and external influences. The changing dynamics in the Middle East signal a new era where American hegemony is no longer guaranteed, and the region's future will be shaped by a broader array of actors and competing interests.

Chapter 7
The Energy Weapon

Energy has long been a strategic commodity, shaping global politics, economies, and power dynamics. In the 21st century, the control and distribution of energy resources have become not just a matter of economic interest but also a tool of geopolitical influence. Countries rich in oil, natural gas, and other energy resources have recognized the potential of using energy as a weapon to achieve political and strategic objectives. Russia, in particular, has mastered the use of energy resources as leverage to exert influence over neighboring countries and rival powers, making energy a cornerstone of its foreign policy strategy. By controlling critical energy supplies and infrastructure, Russia has been able to manipulate the political decisions of European nations, increase its regional dominance, and challenge Western-led sanctions.

For Russia, energy resources are both an economic lifeline and a key instrument of foreign policy. The country is one of the world's largest producers and exporters of natural gas and oil, with much of its energy exports flowing into Europe. Moscow has strategically used its position as a dominant energy supplier to exert pressure on European countries, ensuring that they remain dependent on Russian energy and, by extension, maintain favorable political relationships. This use of energy as leverage has been particularly evident in Russia's control of pipelines that deliver gas to Europe, such as Nord Stream, which runs under the Baltic Sea directly to Germany, bypassing Ukraine. By manipulating energy flows, Russia has been able to coerce countries into aligning with its political interests or face the consequences of energy shortages or price hikes.

The use of the energy weapon is not limited to energy-dependent European countries. Russia's energy influence extends to former Soviet republics and global markets, where the threat of cutting off energy supplies serves as a tool to enforce political alignment and limit Western influence. In this chapter, we explore how Russia has weaponized its vast energy resources, the implications of this strategy for global security, and the broader geopolitical consequences. We will examine the ways in which Russia has employed energy to destabilize regions, undermine political opposition, and assert its dominance in global affairs. Moreover, we will discuss the vulnerabilities this energy dependence creates for countries in Europe, the United States, and beyond, and the global efforts to reduce reliance on Russian energy supplies.

Russia's Control Over European Energy Markets

Russia has long maintained a central role in the global energy landscape, with its vast reserves of natural gas and oil serving as powerful tools of economic and geopolitical leverage. In particular, Russia's control over European energy markets has become a key aspect of its foreign policy, allowing it to exert significant influence over European countries, many of which rely heavily on Russian energy supplies. As the largest natural gas exporter to Europe, Russia has strategically used its energy dominance to shape political dynamics, solidify alliances, and undermine the unity of the European Union (EU) and NATO. This reliance on Russian energy has made Europe vulnerable to manipulation and has complicated efforts to diversify energy sources and reduce dependence on Moscow.

At the heart of Russia's control over European energy markets is its ability to deliver natural gas via a complex network of pipelines that stretch across the continent. The country's natural gas infrastructure is extensive, with pipelines running through Ukraine, Belarus, and the Balkans, as well as more recent projects like the Nord Stream pipelines that run directly from Russia to Germany beneath the Baltic Sea. These pipelines give Russia significant leverage, allowing it to control the flow of gas to multiple European nations, particularly in Central and Eastern Europe, which have limited alternative energy sources. By manipulating the flow of gas—whether through cutting off supplies, adjusting prices, or reducing delivery volumes—Russia can create economic pressure on European countries, forcing them to make political concessions or align more closely with Russia's interests.

The use of energy as a political tool became most apparent during the gas disputes between Russia and Ukraine. In 2006 and 2009, Russia cut off natural gas supplies to Ukraine, which disrupted deliveries to several European countries. These gas supply interruptions highlighted Europe's dependence on Russian energy and exposed the vulnerability of many countries that lacked diversified energy sources. As a result, several EU nations have been forced to reconsider their energy security strategies and find ways to mitigate Russia's influence. However, despite efforts to diversify energy sources through initiatives like the Southern Gas Corridor, which aims to bring gas from the Caspian region to Europe, and renewable energy projects, Russia's control over pipelines like Nord Stream has remained a significant challenge.

Nord Stream, which became operational in 2011, marked a significant step in Russia's strategy to bypass Ukraine and secure a direct route to European markets, particularly Germany, which is the

EU's largest consumer of Russian gas. The Nord Stream 2 pipeline, which is set to double the capacity of the original pipeline, has been a particularly contentious project. While proponents argue that it will ensure a reliable and cost-effective supply of gas to Europe, critics view it as a strategic move by Russia to deepen its hold over European energy markets. The pipeline would further diminish the role of Ukraine as a transit country, undermining its position both economically and politically. Additionally, the pipeline could weaken the EU's collective energy security and divide member states, with some countries, including the U.S., Poland, and Ukraine, strongly opposing the project.

Russia's dominance in European energy markets is also tied to its role as a key supplier of oil. Although Europe's oil supply is more diversified than its natural gas supply, Russia remains one of the largest oil exporters to the continent, particularly to Eastern and Central Europe. Moscow has used this position to exert economic pressure, as it did in 2014 by temporarily halting oil deliveries to Poland and other countries in retaliation for their political alignment with the West. Oil and gas exports are a crucial part of Russia's economy, providing substantial revenue that underpins the Kremlin's ability to exert influence both domestically and internationally. The energy trade also plays a critical role in strengthening Russia's ties with certain European countries, where businesses and political leaders often have significant stakes in Russian energy companies.

Russia's energy dominance has also contributed to its broader strategy of undermining European unity and fostering division within the EU. By cultivating relationships with specific countries, particularly those that are heavily reliant on Russian energy, Russia has been able to drive wedges between EU member states. For example, Russia has used its energy leverage to sway countries like Hungary and Italy, whose leaders have expressed support for closer ties with Moscow. By creating economic dependencies, Russia has been able to exert political influence over these countries, making it more difficult for the EU to adopt a unified stance on key issues such as sanctions against Russia or energy policy.

The weaponization of energy also has implications for NATO, as the alliance's collective security is directly affected by Europe's dependence on Russian gas. Russia has demonstrated its willingness to use energy resources as a means of coercion, and this vulnerability has become a key security concern for NATO members. The potential for energy disruptions, especially in the winter months when demand for heating is highest, highlights the strategic risk posed by Russia's control over energy supplies. As a result, NATO has made energy security a priority, urging member states to diversify their energy sources and reduce their reliance on Russian energy. The alliance has also worked to strengthen energy infrastructure, promote renewable energy, and encourage the development of alternative energy routes to reduce vulnerabilities.

In conclusion, Russia's control over European energy markets represents a potent form of geopolitical leverage. Through its vast network of pipelines, its dominance in natural gas and oil exports, and its ability to manipulate energy flows, Russia has positioned itself as a critical player in Europe's energy security. While efforts have been made to diversify energy sources and reduce dependence on Russian energy, the challenges posed by Russia's control remain significant. This energy leverage continues to shape the political and economic dynamics of Europe, influencing key decisions within the EU and NATO, and highlighting the geopolitical importance of energy security in the 21st century.

Using Gas and Oil as Tools of Power

Russia has long understood the geopolitical leverage it holds through its vast energy resources, particularly oil and natural gas. These energy exports are not merely economic commodities for Russia; they are powerful tools that can be used strategically to achieve political, diplomatic, and military objectives. By leveraging its control over energy supplies, Russia has positioned itself as a critical actor in global energy markets, particularly in Europe, where its energy exports are deeply integrated into the continent's infrastructure. This ability to use oil and gas as tools of power allows Russia to influence both regional and global affairs, challenging Western hegemony and bolstering its own political standing.

The most direct and effective way in which Russia uses oil and gas as instruments of power is through its control over energy supply routes, particularly to Europe. The European Union (EU) is heavily reliant on Russian gas, with Russia providing approximately 40% of the continent's gas imports. This reliance gives Russia the ability to manipulate energy flows and create significant leverage over European countries. Through strategic gas pipelines such as Nord Stream, Yamal, and TurkStream, Russia controls the supply of gas to a number of EU nations, with the capacity to adjust, reduce, or cut off these supplies in times of political tension or crisis. The natural gas supply is particularly crucial for countries like Germany, Italy, and Eastern European nations that depend on Russian energy for heating, electricity generation, and industrial production.

Russia's use of energy as a political tool has been evident in its past actions, particularly in conflicts with Ukraine and Belarus. In 2006 and 2009, Russia used its control over gas supplies to Ukraine as leverage during disputes over gas prices and unpaid debts. These disruptions, while primarily affecting Ukraine, also led to broader gas shortages in Europe, highlighting the vulnerability of EU countries dependent on Russian gas. By cutting off or reducing gas flows to Ukraine, Russia was able to pressure Kyiv into agreeing to terms favorable to Moscow. Similarly, in 2014, Russia reduced gas supplies to Belarus during a dispute over energy pricing, further demonstrating its willingness to use energy resources to coerce neighboring countries. These actions have underscored the extent to which Russia uses energy as a geopolitical weapon, ensuring that countries in its sphere of influence align with its political and economic interests or face the consequences of supply interruptions.

The exploitation of oil and gas also plays a critical role in Russia's relationships with major global powers. Russia's position as one of the largest oil and gas exporters in the world has allowed it to develop strategic partnerships with both developed and developing nations. Countries like China, India, and Turkey, which are key consumers of Russian energy, are strategically important partners for Russia. The Kremlin has used energy exports to build these relationships, offering favorable contracts and energy pricing in exchange for political support. For instance, Russia has signed long-term agreements with China for the delivery of natural gas through the Power of Siberia pipeline, solidifying a growing energy partnership between the two nations. Similarly, Russia's involvement in energy projects with Turkey, including the TurkStream pipeline, has enhanced political cooperation between the two countries, even as their interests diverge on some regional issues.

Energy exports also provide Russia with significant financial resources, which can be used to support its geopolitical ambitions and bolster its military capabilities. Oil and gas revenues make up a large portion of Russia's state budget, allowing the Kremlin to fund its domestic priorities and military expansion. This financial power enables Russia to project its influence globally, whether through military interventions, as seen in Syria, or through political and economic support for allies in the Middle East and Central Asia. The Kremlin has been able to exert influence over countries like Iran, Venezuela, and Syria by using energy deals as a form of financial and political backing, ensuring that these nations align with Russian interests and provide support in international forums.

Moreover, Russia has increasingly used its energy resources to challenge the liberal international order and undermine Western sanctions. By diversifying its energy trade routes, particularly through the construction of new pipelines like Nord Stream 2, Russia has sought to reduce its dependence on traditional transit routes that pass through Ukraine and Central Europe, making it less vulnerable to external pressure. These pipelines also offer Russia an opportunity to bypass the EU's collective decision-making on energy issues, thus enabling it to exert more direct control over its energy dealings with key European countries. The ability to circumvent Western sanctions by leveraging energy resources has allowed Russia to continue strengthening its position while simultaneously undermining efforts by the EU and the U.S. to isolate Russia economically.

In conclusion, Russia's use of gas and oil as tools of power represents a highly effective strategy that enables it to shape global geopolitics, secure its regional dominance, and challenge Western influence. Through control over energy supplies, Russia can manipulate political decisions, create dependencies, and ensure that countries align with its interests, all while generating significant revenue to support its broader geopolitical goals. Energy resources are central to Russia's foreign policy, serving as both an economic driver and a means of asserting its power on the global stage. As the world continues to navigate the complexities of energy transitions and regional conflicts, Russia's ability to leverage oil and gas will remain a critical element in its strategic approach to global influence.

The Impact on Global Energy Dynamics

Russia's strategic use of oil and natural gas as tools of geopolitical power has had profound implications for global energy dynamics, particularly in Europe and the wider international market. As one of the largest energy producers in the world, Russia's influence in the global energy sector goes far beyond simply being a supplier. Its ability to manipulate energy flows and control key infrastructure has reshaped energy relationships, introduced new vulnerabilities for consumers, and given rise to new alliances and rivalries. Russia's control over energy supplies has become a central factor in the evolution of global energy markets, and its influence will likely continue to be a determining factor in how energy policy is formulated in both the short and long term.

One of the most significant impacts of Russia's energy dominance has been felt in Europe, where many countries are heavily dependent on Russian oil and gas. This dependency has made Europe vulnerable to geopolitical pressures, as Russia has the ability to disrupt energy supplies to force political concessions. For instance, during the gas disputes between Russia and Ukraine in 2006 and 2009, Russia cut off natural gas supplies to Ukraine, which in turn led to shortages in other European countries. These interruptions exposed Europe's overreliance on Russian energy and highlighted the lack of energy security within the EU. Russia's ability to control key gas pipelines, such as the Yamal and Nord Stream pipelines, has allowed it to bypass traditional transit routes and impose additional leverage on countries that rely on energy imports. In response to these vulnerabilities, the European Union has sought to diversify its energy sources through projects like the Southern Gas Corridor, which aims to bring natural gas from Azerbaijan and other sources to Europe, reducing reliance on Russia.

Furthermore, Russia's energy leverage has driven significant shifts in the international oil and gas markets. By investing in long-term contracts and forming strategic alliances with countries like China, India, and Turkey, Russia has effectively strengthened its position in the global energy trade. China, in particular, has become one of Russia's most important energy partners. Through initiatives like the Power of Siberia pipeline, Russia has sought to secure a growing market for its natural gas, balancing the European market with a growing demand from Asia. This shift has allowed Russia to maintain its relevance as a global energy supplier, despite increasing pressure from Western sanctions and efforts to reduce its influence in Europe. The diversification of Russia's energy export destinations has reduced its vulnerability to Western pressure, but it has also created new dynamics in global energy competition, especially as China becomes more assertive in its demand for energy.

Russia's role in the global energy market is also critical in the context of the OPEC+ arrangement, which involves a coalition of oil-producing nations working together to control production levels and influence global oil prices. As a leading non-OPEC member, Russia plays an influential role in shaping oil production quotas, especially in times of market instability. The cooperation between Russia and Saudi Arabia, as part of the OPEC+ agreement, has allowed both countries to manage oil production and influence global prices. This partnership, which began in 2016, has made Russia an essential player in global oil markets, further cementing its role as a key global energy power. Russia's ability to influence global oil production, through its alliances with OPEC countries, has allowed it to secure favorable economic outcomes while also shaping energy policies on a global scale.

On the flip side, Russia's energy dominance has driven countries to seek alternatives and reduce their dependence on Russian supplies. In Europe, the diversification of energy sources has been a growing priority, with the EU investing in renewable energy, energy efficiency, and alternative natural gas suppliers. Projects such as the Trans Adriatic Pipeline (TAP) and the construction of floating LNG terminals in countries like Lithuania are part of broader efforts to reduce reliance on Russian energy. In addition, some European countries have increased their focus on renewable energy sources, such as wind, solar, and nuclear power, to diversify their energy mix and enhance energy security. These efforts have been part of the broader European Green Deal, aimed at reducing carbon emissions and addressing the challenges of climate change, but they also serve as a countermeasure to Russia's energy dominance.

The geopolitical implications of Russia's role in the global energy market extend beyond Europe and Asia, influencing global energy dynamics more broadly. Russia's ability to use energy as leverage has made it a central player in broader geopolitical struggles, particularly in the Middle East, where it has formed alliances with key oil producers and energy consumers. Russia's involvement in countries like Syria and Iran has allowed it to exert influence over regional energy flows, while its alliances with oil-rich countries have bolstered its political and economic influence in key areas. These energy-based partnerships have extended Russia's reach, enabling it to challenge Western interests and limit the influence of the U.S. and its allies in the region.

Moreover, Russia's use of energy as a tool of power has spurred competition from other global energy producers. The U.S., through its shale oil and gas revolution, has emerged as a major competitor to Russia in global energy markets. The increased production of liquefied natural gas (LNG) in the U.S. has allowed it to challenge Russia's dominance in both European and Asian markets. Similarly, Middle Eastern countries like Qatar, Saudi Arabia, and the UAE are also diversifying their energy exports, creating alternative sources of supply and further reducing the influence of Russia.

In conclusion, Russia's control over global energy markets has had far-reaching impacts, both regionally and globally. Through its manipulation of energy supply routes, partnerships with key energy consumers, and strategic involvement in global energy organizations, Russia has positioned itself as a key geopolitical player. However, its energy leverage has also driven efforts to diversify energy sources and reduce dependence on Russian supplies, reshaping the global energy landscape. As the world transitions to cleaner energy and seeks to reduce reliance on fossil fuels, the future of Russia's energy dominance will be influenced by the growing competition from alternative sources and the global shift toward sustainability. Nonetheless, Russia's ability to use energy as a geopolitical tool will remain a critical factor in shaping global energy dynamics for the foreseeable future.

Chapter 8
Economic War: Sanctions and Countermeasures

In the modern geopolitical landscape, economic sanctions have become one of the most widely used tools of foreign policy, allowing countries to exert pressure without resorting to military conflict. Russia, in particular, has found itself at the center of this economic warfare, as Western nations, particularly the United States and the European Union, have increasingly imposed sanctions in response to Moscow's actions in Ukraine, Syria, and its alleged interference in democratic processes abroad. Sanctions are designed to isolate Russia economically, disrupt its financial systems, and limit its access to global markets and resources, forcing the Kremlin to reconsider its geopolitical ambitions. However, while these sanctions have certainly had a significant impact on Russia's economy, they have also prompted Russia to develop a series of countermeasures that have reshaped its economy and its relationship with the global market.

Russia's response to Western sanctions has been multifaceted, ranging from efforts to diversify its economy and reduce its reliance on foreign capital, to the development of new trade partnerships and alternative financial systems. One of the key aspects of Russia's counter-sanctions strategy has been the push for economic self-sufficiency. This has involved the creation of import substitution programs, which aim to replace foreign goods with domestically produced alternatives. Russia has also sought to strengthen its ties with countries outside the West, particularly China, India, and several nations in the Middle East and Africa. These new alliances have allowed Russia to access markets that are less affected by Western sanctions and to reduce its dependency on the European Union and the United States for trade and investment.

Despite these efforts, Russia's ability to withstand the economic pressure of Western sanctions is still a subject of debate. While the sanctions have undoubtedly caused economic hardship, particularly in the energy sector, they have also spurred innovation and forced Russia to rethink its economic and geopolitical strategies. This chapter explores the complex dynamics of economic warfare, examining how sanctions and countermeasures have reshaped Russia's economic landscape, and the broader implications of this economic conflict for global trade, finance, and diplomacy. We will analyze the effectiveness of sanctions, the resilience of Russia's economy, and how these economic battles are playing out in the context of Russia's broader geopolitical objectives.

America's Sanctions Against Russia: Effectiveness and Limitations

The United States has imposed a series of economic sanctions against Russia over the past decade, aimed at punishing Moscow for a range of actions including its annexation of Crimea in 2014, its interference in the 2016 U.S. presidential election, and its military involvement in Syria, among other issues. These sanctions have been a cornerstone of U.S. foreign policy toward Russia, reflecting an effort to isolate the country diplomatically and economically in response to its increasingly aggressive actions on the global stage. The objective behind these sanctions is to pressure the Russian government to alter its behavior, particularly its foreign policy actions, while also signaling to the international community the U.S.'s commitment to defending the global order and its allies.

The sanctions imposed on Russia by the U.S. fall into several categories: financial restrictions, export controls, asset freezes, and sectoral sanctions. Financial sanctions target major Russian banks, limiting their access to U.S. dollars and international capital markets. Export controls restrict the sale of high-tech goods and services, particularly in sectors critical to Russia's modernization efforts, such as the energy and defense industries. Asset freezes prevent key individuals, including oligarchs and government officials close to President Vladimir Putin, from accessing their financial assets abroad. Sectoral sanctions aim to limit Russia's access to advanced technology, particularly in the energy sector, where Western companies control much of the technology used in oil and gas exploration. Collectively, these sanctions were designed to strangle Russia's economy, limit its global influence, and weaken its political leadership.

The effectiveness of these sanctions has been a subject of considerable debate. On one hand, the sanctions have succeeded in creating significant economic pain for Russia. The Russian economy shrank in the wake of the 2014 sanctions, and its currency, the ruble, plummeted in value. The sanctions have isolated Russia from key international financial markets and reduced foreign direct investment, which had been flowing into the country before the crisis in Ukraine. Additionally, the sanctions on Russia's energy sector have made it more difficult for Russia to access advanced technology for oil and gas exploration, which has stymied its ability to develop new energy projects and tapped into potential reserves. The decline in oil prices in 2014, coupled with sanctions, dealt a heavy blow to Russia's economy, which relies heavily on energy exports for revenue.

However, the sanctions have not produced the desired political change within Russia. Despite the economic consequences, the Russian government has remained largely resilient. In fact, many analysts argue that the sanctions have only strengthened Putin's grip on power by rallying domestic support under the banner of nationalism. The Kremlin has used the sanctions as a rallying point, framing them as an unjust attack on Russia by the West, and this narrative has helped consolidate Putin's political standing within the country. Furthermore, Russia's leadership has taken steps to reduce its dependence on Western financial systems and diversify its trade relationships, particularly with China and other non-Western countries. These moves have allowed Russia to mitigate some of the worst effects of the sanctions, allowing it to remain a key player in global energy markets, even while under pressure.

The limitations of the sanctions are also evident in their failure to significantly alter Russian foreign policy or bring about a change in its actions in Ukraine, Syria, or other regions. Moscow has continued its support for Bashar al-Assad in Syria, engaged in destabilizing activities in Ukraine, and maintained its aggressive stance toward NATO and the EU. Despite the economic costs, Russia has not been compelled to make the necessary concessions that the sanctions were intended to force. Part of the reason for this is that Russia's leadership has increasingly turned toward alternative markets and financing options, particularly in Asia. The growing economic ties between Russia and China, for instance, have allowed Moscow to circumvent some of the limitations imposed by Western sanctions, particularly in energy markets. Additionally, Russia has invested heavily in developing domestic alternatives to Western technologies and financial systems, reducing its vulnerability to sanctions.

Another limitation of U.S. sanctions is the uneven implementation and support for them within the international community. While many Western allies have joined in imposing sanctions on Russia, some countries have been reluctant to fully implement them or have found ways to bypass them. For example, countries like India, Turkey, and some European nations have maintained economic relationships with Russia, particularly in energy trade, and have at times opposed further sanctions or diluted their impact. This lack of unanimous global support has allowed Russia to find alternative trading partners and financing sources, undermining the effectiveness of the sanctions.

Moreover, the sanctions' long-term impact on Russia's economy has been mixed. While they have certainly contributed to economic stagnation, they have not led to the kind of collapse that might force a political shift. Russia has pursued a policy of "import substitution," developing domestic alternatives to goods that were previously imported from the West, particularly in agriculture and defense sectors. While this has had some success, it has not been sufficient to fully offset the negative effects of the sanctions. Russia has also turned to China for investment and trade, further shifting its economic orientation away from Europe and the U.S.

In conclusion, while U.S. sanctions on Russia have had a significant economic impact, they have proven to be only partially effective in achieving their intended political goals. The sanctions have caused economic hardship, isolated Russia from Western markets, and limited its access to advanced technologies, particularly in the energy sector. However, they have not led to the political changes that the West hoped for, and Russia has managed to adapt to the economic pressure by diversifying its trade relationships and reducing its reliance on Western systems. The limitations of the sanctions, combined with Russia's resilience and strategic countermeasures, suggest that economic warfare, while an important tool in foreign policy, has its boundaries in the case of a determined and resourceful adversary like Russia.

Russia's Economic Resilience and Workarounds

Despite facing crippling international sanctions and economic pressures, Russia has demonstrated a remarkable ability to adapt, leveraging its economic resilience and implementing a range of workarounds to mitigate the negative effects. These workarounds have allowed Russia to continue pursuing its geopolitical and economic objectives, even as the country navigates a more isolated position on the global stage. While sanctions imposed by the U.S. and European Union have undoubtedly caused significant economic disruption, particularly in sectors like energy, finance, and technology, Russia's ability to diversify its economic relationships, bolster its domestic industries, and innovate its financial systems has enabled it to weather many of the storms.

One of the primary strategies that Russia has employed to counteract the impact of Western sanctions is the diversification of its trade relationships. Faced with limited access to European and U.S. markets, Russia has increasingly turned to non-Western countries, particularly China, India, and other nations in the Middle East, for trade and investment opportunities. China, in particular, has become Russia's most important economic partner. The two countries have significantly strengthened their economic ties, with China becoming a major buyer of Russian energy exports, including oil, natural gas, and coal. The Power of Siberia pipeline, which began operations in December 2019, is a key component of this relationship, enabling Russia to supply China with natural gas, further solidifying their economic partnership. Additionally, Russia has used its energy resources as leverage to forge closer relationships with India and other countries in Asia, compensating for the loss of European customers.

In addition to strengthening relationships with non-Western powers, Russia has sought to reduce its reliance on Western financial systems and institutions. The 2014 sanctions, which targeted Russia's access to international financial markets, led to a concerted effort by the Russian government to develop domestic financial alternatives. One of the most significant measures taken was the creation of Russia's own payment system, known as the MIR payment system, which was designed to replace Western payment networks like Visa and MasterCard. The MIR system allows Russian consumers and businesses to continue making payments both domestically and internationally, circumventing the reliance on foreign financial networks. Russia has also worked to build up its foreign exchange reserves, which now stand at over $600 billion, providing a cushion against the effects of sanctions and economic instability. This financial autonomy has helped Russia to avoid some of the worst consequences of Western financial sanctions.

Another significant workaround that Russia has implemented to mitigate the effects of sanctions is the promotion of import substitution. Import substitution refers to the strategy of replacing foreign imports with domestically produced goods in order to reduce the country's dependency on external suppliers. The Russian government has heavily invested in this strategy, particularly in sectors such as agriculture, defense, and technology. For example, after Western countries imposed sanctions on Russian agricultural products, including food and drinks, Russia responded by ramping up domestic production. Russian farmers began cultivating more crops, and the country became more self-sufficient in many agricultural products, such as grains, dairy, and meat. This shift has had a positive impact on Russia's agricultural sector, which is now one of the fastest-growing parts of the economy.

In the defense sector, Russia has used import substitution to reduce its reliance on Western technologies, particularly in advanced military hardware and components. Despite facing sanctions that restrict its access to high-tech military components, Russia has managed to maintain and expand its defense capabilities through domestic production and the development of indigenous technologies. Russian defense companies have worked to create alternatives to foreign parts, ensuring that the country can maintain its military readiness despite restrictions on imports. Additionally, Russia has looked to China and other countries for military technology transfers and collaboration, further diversifying its defense partnerships.

The energy sector, which is the cornerstone of Russia's economy, has also benefited from workarounds in the face of sanctions. While Russia has been affected by sanctions targeting its energy projects, it has continued to find new ways to assert its dominance in global energy markets. Russia has pursued new energy routes, such as the Nord Stream 2 pipeline, which is designed to deliver natural gas directly to Germany, bypassing Ukraine and Central European countries. The pipeline has faced significant opposition from the U.S. and some EU members, but it has remained a critical element of Russia's strategy to secure its energy exports to Europe. Additionally, Russia has increased its focus on liquefied natural gas (LNG) production, which has enabled it to supply gas to countries outside of Europe, particularly in Asia. As the global LNG market grows, Russia has positioned itself as a key player, supplying energy to countries like China, Japan, and South Korea.

Russia has also worked to strengthen its domestic industrial base, focusing on sectors such as high-tech industries, telecommunications, and manufacturing. While Russia still faces challenges in terms of technological development, it has made strides in areas such as software development, military technology, and aerospace. The government has provided incentives for Russian companies to develop and produce high-tech products, which reduces the reliance on imports from the West. This strategy has been particularly important in the face of sanctions that target Russia's access to advanced technologies. By fostering innovation and increasing domestic production, Russia is building a more self-reliant economy that is less vulnerable to external pressures.

In conclusion, Russia's economic resilience in the face of sanctions can be attributed to its strategic diversification of trade relationships, the development of domestic financial systems, the promotion of import substitution, and its continued dominance in the energy sector. While the sanctions have undoubtedly caused economic hardship, Russia's ability to adapt and find workarounds has allowed it to maintain a degree of stability and continue pursuing its geopolitical objectives. As global power dynamics shift and the impact of sanctions evolves, Russia's capacity to navigate economic challenges will remain a crucial factor in its continued influence on the global stage.

The Shift Towards Economic Alliances in the East

In recent years, Russia has increasingly shifted its focus toward strengthening economic alliances in the East, particularly with China, India, and other countries in Asia, as part of a strategic effort to reduce its reliance on the West and mitigate the impact of Western sanctions. This pivot to the East reflects broader global geopolitical trends, where economic power and influence are increasingly concentrated in Asia. As Russia faces ongoing economic pressure from the U.S. and the European Union due to sanctions, it has sought to diversify its trade relationships, deepen economic integration with emerging markets, and capitalize on the growing demand for energy and infrastructure development in the East. This shift marks a new chapter in Russia's foreign policy, as it positions itself as a key player in the evolving economic landscape of Asia.

China, by far the most significant partner in Russia's eastern pivot, has become the cornerstone of Russia's new economic strategy. The bilateral trade relationship between Russia and China has expanded rapidly in recent years, driven largely by Russia's vast energy resources and China's growing demand for energy to fuel its industrialization and economic growth. China is now the largest importer of Russian oil, natural gas, and coal, and Russia has increasingly become a vital supplier of energy to China. One of the key projects in this relationship is the Power of Siberia pipeline, which began operating in December 2019, delivering natural gas from Russia to China. This pipeline represents not only an important economic deal but also a strategic partnership that strengthens Russia's energy export base while reducing its reliance on European markets. Additionally, the two countries have expanded their economic ties in areas such as defense, high technology, and infrastructure development. China's Belt and Road Initiative (BRI), which seeks to enhance trade and connectivity across Asia, Europe, and Africa, presents a unique opportunity for Russia to integrate more deeply into Asia's economic networks and benefit from infrastructure investments.

Russia's growing economic relationship with China is also part of a broader shift in the global economic order, where Asia, driven by China's economic rise, is becoming the focal point of international trade and investment. The shift toward Asia reflects Russia's desire to align itself with the economic powerhouse of the East, which is expected to play a dominant role in the global economy in the coming decades. In doing so, Russia is positioning itself as a key partner in the development of new trade routes, energy infrastructure, and supply chains, while reducing its vulnerability to economic isolation from the West.

India is another critical partner for Russia in the East, with longstanding historical ties and mutual interests in defense, energy, and economic cooperation. India is one of Russia's largest customers for defense technology, particularly in the areas of air defense systems, fighter jets, and military hardware. The two countries have also been working to deepen their economic ties, particularly in the energy sector. Russia is a key supplier of oil and natural gas to India, and the two countries have been exploring opportunities for greater cooperation in the areas of nuclear energy, infrastructure, and technology. India's rapidly growing economy, coupled with its strategic position in Asia, makes it an important player in Russia's efforts to establish a more diversified and balanced set of economic partnerships. Russia's relationship with India is particularly valuable as it provides an alternative to China, which has increasingly dominated the economic landscape in Asia.

Beyond China and India, Russia has been actively cultivating relationships with other countries in the region, including Japan, South Korea, and several nations in Southeast Asia. Russia's engagement with Japan, for example, has focused on energy cooperation, with Russia supplying natural gas and oil to Japan, and Japan offering advanced technology and infrastructure investment in Russia's Far East. Similarly, South Korea and Russia have explored joint ventures in areas such as energy, technology, and transport infrastructure, while Southeast Asia has become an increasingly important market for Russian arms, energy, and agricultural products. Russia's efforts to diversify its economic alliances in the East are not just about building new trade routes or securing new markets; they also reflect the broader goal of integrating Russia into Asia's economic growth and reducing its dependence on Western markets and financial systems.

This shift toward economic alliances in the East is not without its challenges. While Russia has made significant strides in strengthening ties with China and other Asian powers, there are underlying tensions that could complicate these relationships. For instance, Russia's close relationship with China, while economically beneficial, raises concerns over the potential for overdependence on Beijing, particularly in areas such as energy and defense. Some critics argue that Russia risks becoming too aligned with China's economic and political agenda, undermining its sovereignty and ability to act independently on the global stage. Similarly, Russia's efforts to engage with India, Japan, and other regional players must be carefully balanced, as these countries have their own competing interests and relationships with the West.

Despite these challenges, Russia's shift toward the East represents a strategic pivot that allows the country to diversify its economic relationships, increase its influence in the rapidly growing economies of Asia, and reduce its vulnerability to the economic isolation imposed by the West. As global economic power continues to shift toward Asia, Russia's deepening ties with China, India, and other key players in the region will play a central role in shaping the future of global trade, energy markets, and geopolitical dynamics. This shift is not just an economic necessity for Russia; it is also a key component of its broader strategy to reshape its place in the global order and secure its interests in an increasingly multipolar world.

Chapter 9
Russia and China: The Strategic Partnership

The strategic partnership between Russia and China has emerged as one of the most significant geopolitical developments of the 21st century, reshaping the global balance of power. Although the two nations have historically had complex and sometimes adversarial relationships, in recent years they have increasingly aligned their interests, forming a robust alliance that challenges the traditional influence of the West. This partnership is not only defined by economic cooperation but also by shared geopolitical objectives, military collaboration, and mutual concerns over the growing dominance of the United States. As Russia seeks to diversify its economic relationships away from the West and China continues its rise as an economic and military superpower, the two nations have found common ground in addressing global challenges and pursuing their strategic goals.

At the heart of the Russia-China relationship lies an economic alliance that has flourished in the wake of sanctions and shifting global markets. Russia, with its vast natural resources, has become a critical energy supplier to China, which is the world's largest importer of oil and gas. The development of key infrastructure projects, such as the Power of Siberia pipeline and the growing network of trade routes under China's Belt and Road Initiative (BRI), has solidified their economic ties. In return, China has provided

Russia with much-needed investment in sectors such as technology, manufacturing, and infrastructure, helping Russia to reduce its dependence on Western economies. This economic cooperation has provided both countries with the opportunity to balance their reliance on the West while ensuring their continued growth in a rapidly changing global landscape.

Beyond economic collaboration, the Russia-China strategic partnership has deepened in military and security cooperation, driven by shared concerns over U.S. global hegemony and the potential threat of Western influence in their respective regions. The two countries have held joint military exercises, expanded defense cooperation, and supported each other in international forums, particularly in the United Nations Security Council. Their alignment on issues such as countering Western sanctions, resisting foreign intervention, and maintaining sovereignty in the face of external pressure has positioned them as two of the most influential voices in global affairs. This chapter explores the multifaceted nature of the Russia-China strategic partnership, examining how it has evolved, the interests it serves, and the broader implications it has for global power dynamics.

The Growth of the Russia-China Alliance

The Russia-China alliance has evolved from a historically cautious relationship to one of the most strategic partnerships in global geopolitics. Over the past two decades, this alliance has grown in both scope and depth, driven by mutual economic, geopolitical, and security interests. While the two countries' relationship has been shaped by periods of tension, particularly during the Cold War, their growing alignment is a result of changing global power dynamics, the rise of China as an economic powerhouse, and Russia's increasing isolation from the West. The partnership between Russia and China is now characterized by cooperation across multiple domains—economic, political, military, and cultural—making it one of the most significant strategic alignments in the 21st century.

The foundation of the Russia-China alliance lies in shared economic interests, particularly in energy and infrastructure. Russia, with its vast natural resources, is a crucial supplier of oil, natural gas, and other commodities to China, the world's second-largest economy. In recent years, Russia has focused on strengthening its economic ties with China to reduce its dependency on Western markets, especially after facing sanctions from the United States and European Union. Energy has become a central pillar of their cooperation, and one of the landmark projects is the Power of Siberia gas pipeline, which began operating in December 2019, transporting natural gas from Russia to China. This pipeline represents not only a major economic partnership but also a geopolitical shift, as it diversifies China's energy sources and reduces its reliance on more traditional energy partners like the Middle East. Furthermore, the China-led Belt and Road Initiative (BRI), which seeks to improve global trade routes, has opened up new avenues for Russia to connect with China and other countries in Asia, Europe, and Africa. Russia has positioned itself as a key participant in the BRI, ensuring that its economic integration with China extends beyond energy and into infrastructure, trade, and technology.

On the political front, both Russia and China share common interests in opposing U.S. global dominance and resisting what they perceive as Western interference in their domestic affairs. Russia, in particular, has been a vocal critic of U.S. foreign policy, particularly after its annexation of Crimea in 2014 and the subsequent sanctions that were imposed by the West. Similarly, China has grown increasingly wary of U.S. policies, especially with regard to trade disputes, the South China Sea, and Taiwan. Both nations have used their strategic partnership to counterbalance U.S. influence in international organizations and in regional affairs. At the United Nations Security Council, both Russia and China have worked together to veto resolutions that they view as unfavorable to their national interests, such as those related to Syria and North Korea. Their alignment at the UN reflects their shared goal of maintaining a multipolar world order, where no single country or bloc can dominate global decision-making. This political synergy allows them to present a united front on issues of global governance and regional stability, challenging Western-led institutions and norms.

In terms of military cooperation, the Russia-China alliance has witnessed significant growth, with both countries conducting joint military exercises and expanding defense collaboration. Although the two nations do not have a formal military alliance like NATO, their growing military ties reflect their shared concerns over security issues. Both Russia and China are wary of U.S. military presence in their respective regions—Russia in Eastern Europe and China in the Asia-Pacific—and have coordinated their efforts to push back against Western influence. They have held joint military drills, such as the Vostok and Tsentr exercises, which simulate large-scale operations and serve as a demonstration of their military capabilities. Additionally, Russia has provided China with advanced military technology, including air defense systems and fighter jets, further deepening their defense cooperation. This military alignment has not only strengthened their bilateral ties but also altered the security dynamics in the Asia-Pacific region and beyond, presenting a challenge to U.S. military dominance.

The alliance also extends to other areas of cooperation, including technology, space exploration, and cultural exchange. In the field of technology, China and Russia have collaborated on joint ventures in sectors like telecommunications, artificial intelligence, and cybersecurity. Russia's efforts to build alternative technologies and systems that are not reliant on Western corporations align with China's goal of reducing its dependence on foreign technology, particularly in areas like 5G networks. In space exploration, both countries have cooperated on projects such as the Russian-made engines used in China's space missions. These collaborations not only boost their technological capabilities but also serve as a counterweight to the West's dominance in these high-tech sectors.

The growth of the Russia-China alliance is not without challenges. While both nations share common interests in countering U.S. influence, they also have distinct national agendas. Russia is wary of becoming too dependent on China, particularly in areas like energy and military technology, as it risks losing its strategic autonomy. Similarly, China's growing global influence sometimes leads to concerns in Russia about being overshadowed by its more powerful partner. However, despite these challenges, both countries have managed to navigate their differences and build a partnership that benefits both sides. Russia provides China with critical energy resources and military technology, while China offers Russia access to an expanding market, investment opportunities, and advanced technological developments.

In conclusion, the Russia-China alliance has grown into a strategic partnership that transcends economic, political, and military cooperation. Both countries share common interests in countering Western influence, and their growing alignment reflects a broader shift in global power dynamics, where Asia is increasingly becoming the center of economic and geopolitical activity. As China continues to rise as an economic and military superpower, Russia stands to gain from its deepening partnership with Beijing. Together, they are reshaping the global order, challenging the dominance of the U.S. and its allies, and building a multipolar world where their influence is key. The growth of this alliance will likely be a defining feature of global geopolitics in the coming decades.

The Military and Economic Synergies

The military and economic synergies between Russia and China have become central to their growing strategic partnership, positioning the two countries as formidable players on the global stage. Their alliance is not merely transactional but instead reflects a shared vision of challenging Western dominance, particularly that of the United States, and reshaping the international order to better suit their national interests. By harmonizing their military capabilities and economic resources, Russia and China have been able to create a powerful, multifaceted alliance that has significant implications for global security, trade, and geopolitical dynamics.

From a military perspective, the Russia-China alliance has witnessed increasing collaboration in defense, both in terms of joint exercises and the sharing of military technologies. While the two countries do not have a formal military alliance akin to NATO, they have increasingly cooperated in various defense sectors, signaling a deeper strategic alignment. One of the most visible expressions of this cooperation is their joint military exercises, such as the "Vostok" and "Tsentr" drills. These exercises simulate large-scale military operations, with both Russian and Chinese forces working together in complex maneuvers that emphasize interoperability and shared defense strategies. These exercises are a demonstration of their growing military capabilities and mutual intent to strengthen their defense postures in the face of external pressures, particularly from the U.S. and NATO.

Furthermore, Russia's role as a key supplier of advanced military technologies has significantly bolstered China's defense capabilities. Moscow has provided China with a range of critical military equipment, including air defense systems like the S-400 and advanced fighter jets, such as the Su-35. These systems enhance China's military power, particularly in the Asia-Pacific region, where U.S. military presence remains a concern for Beijing. In return, China has been a significant purchaser of Russian weapons and military hardware, which not only strengthens China's defense but also supports Russia's economy, which relies on arms exports. This mutually beneficial defense cooperation enables both nations to modernize their militaries and project power on the global stage, while also sending a message of unity and strength to their geopolitical rivals.

On the economic front, the synergies between Russia and China are similarly substantial. The economic ties between the two countries have deepened considerably, particularly in energy trade, infrastructure development, and technology exchange. China is Russia's largest trading partner, and Russia plays a crucial role in China's energy security. The two countries have solidified this partnership through major projects like the Power of Siberia pipeline, which allows Russia to export natural gas directly to China, bypassing traditional transit routes through Europe. This energy collaboration serves both countries' strategic goals—Russia gains a stable and growing market for its natural gas exports, while China secures a reliable source of energy to fuel its growing industrial economy. This pipeline is a symbol of the strong economic ties that have emerged from their strategic partnership, which also extends to other energy sources, including oil and coal.

The economic synergies also extend beyond energy. Russia and China have increasingly cooperated in infrastructure development, particularly through China's Belt and Road Initiative (BRI), which aims to connect countries through trade routes and investments in infrastructure. Russia's position at the heart of the BRI offers it the opportunity to be a key player in connecting China to Europe, Central Asia, and the Middle East. Russian participation in BRI projects, including rail and road networks, port construction, and logistics hubs, helps to integrate Russia more deeply into China's economic orbit. This not only boosts Russia's economy but also positions it as a critical partner in the vast economic network that China is building.

In addition to trade and infrastructure, Russia and China have increasingly collaborated in high-tech industries. Russia, facing restrictions on accessing Western technologies due to sanctions, has looked to China for technological support and investment. This partnership has been particularly important in areas such as telecommunications, where Chinese companies like Huawei have provided advanced 5G technology and infrastructure to Russia. In return, Russia has offered China access to its aerospace technologies and other specialized industrial capabilities. The cooperation between the two nations in this domain not only strengthens their economies but also reduces their reliance on Western technology, further solidifying their economic autonomy.

The combined military and economic synergies between Russia and China offer both countries a strategic advantage in the face of global challenges. Together, they challenge U.S. dominance, particularly in the Asia-Pacific region, and create an alternative to the

Western-led global order. Their growing partnership allows them to coordinate on key international issues, such as global trade, security, and diplomatic relations. The alignment of their military and economic interests creates a comprehensive strategy for both nations, positioning them as a powerful bloc that can counterbalance Western influence and project their values and priorities on the global stage.

However, while the synergies between Russia and China have been fruitful, challenges remain. The asymmetry of their relationship—China's economic and military dominance compared to Russia's regional power—can sometimes create tensions, particularly regarding issues of influence and dependence. Nonetheless, the shared strategic goals of challenging the U.S. and reshaping global governance have allowed these challenges to be managed, with both countries focusing on mutual benefits rather than rivalry.

In conclusion, the military and economic synergies between Russia and China are central to their strategic partnership, and these synergies significantly alter global power dynamics. By collaborating militarily and economically, both nations have strengthened their position on the global stage, increasing their ability to influence international affairs. This partnership not only reshapes the geopolitical landscape but also highlights the growing influence of non-Western powers in global governance and security. As Russia and China continue to deepen their ties, their combined power will likely play an increasingly central role in shaping the future of global politics and economics.

Implications for America's Global Position

The growing strategic partnership between Russia and China presents significant implications for America's global position, altering the dynamics of international power, security, and economic influence. As the two countries strengthen their military and economic ties, they pose a formidable challenge to U.S. leadership on the global stage. This partnership, driven by shared geopolitical interests, particularly in countering U.S. dominance and the liberal international order, has the potential to reshape the global balance of power. For America, the emergence of a united Russia-China alliance signals a shift toward a more multipolar world, where its influence is increasingly contested by rising powers in Asia and Eurasia.

One of the most direct implications for the United States is the potential erosion of its geopolitical dominance, particularly in regions where it has historically held significant influence, such as Europe and the Asia-Pacific. In Europe, Russia's increasing collaboration with China, along with its military presence and energy leverage, poses a challenge to U.S. influence in NATO and its ability to act as the primary security guarantor for European countries. Russia's military capabilities, combined with China's growing economic and technological power, create a potent strategic bloc that can counterbalance Western influence in the region. If Russia and China continue to align their efforts to challenge U.S. policy, it may result in a diminished ability for the U.S. to dictate terms on security issues in Europe and force it to adopt a more conciliatory or strategic approach toward both powers.

In the Asia-Pacific region, the Russia-China alliance further complicates U.S. efforts to maintain dominance. China's rise as an economic and military powerhouse has already posed a strategic challenge to the U.S., particularly with regard to its policies in the South China Sea and its growing military presence. The deepening ties between Russia and China, particularly in defense and energy, offer China greater leverage against U.S. influence in the region. Joint military exercises and coordination between the two countries, such as those conducted in the East China Sea and the Russian Far East, present a direct challenge to U.S. military power and its security interests in the region. The United States, already facing a shift in the global power dynamic due to China's economic growth, now faces a two-front challenge in containing both Russia's actions in Eastern Europe and China's aggressive posture in the Pacific.

Economically, the strengthening of the Russia-China alliance presents significant challenges for U.S. interests as well. The two countries have developed robust economic synergies, particularly in energy trade, infrastructure development, and technology exchange. Russia, for example, has emerged as a key supplier of energy to China, especially in the form of natural gas via the Power of Siberia pipeline. This partnership enables both countries to bypass Western-dominated financial institutions and trade routes, creating a new economic axis outside of the U.S.-led global economic system. The Belt and Road Initiative (BRI), which connects China with Eurasian countries, including Russia, has allowed for new infrastructure investments and trade routes that reduce reliance on traditional Western economic hubs. As China's economic influence continues to grow, and with Russia playing a central role in this expansion, the U.S. faces an increasingly competitive environment for global trade, investment, and infrastructure development.

Moreover, the growing Russia-China partnership has led to a shift in the global energy market. The U.S. has been a leader in the global oil and gas industry, but with Russia and China now becoming more closely integrated in their energy production and trade, the U.S. risks losing influence over global energy prices and supply chains. Russia's vast energy resources, combined with China's demand, have positioned the two nations to challenge U.S. dominance in this critical sector. Additionally, as China continues to grow as a technological and economic power, it has begun to reduce its reliance on Western systems, including financial platforms and technological infrastructure. The proliferation of Chinese-developed 5G networks, for example, represents a growing challenge to American tech companies and a new area of competition for global dominance.

In terms of global governance, the Russia-China alliance has implications for the U.S.'s ability to lead international organizations and shape the global rules-based order. Both countries have increasingly sought to challenge U.S. influence in the United Nations, the World Trade Organization, and other multilateral institutions. At the U.N., Russia and China have often collaborated to veto resolutions that they view as threatening to their interests, such as those related to Syria or North Korea. This alignment has reduced the U.S.'s ability to shape outcomes in these international bodies and has given Russia and China a larger voice in global decision-making. As both countries promote an alternative vision of international governance—one that emphasizes state sovereignty, non-interference, and multipolarity—the U.S. faces the growing challenge of defending its values and interests in a rapidly shifting geopolitical landscape.

The implications for America's global position are also felt in the realm of cybersecurity and information warfare. The growing technological cooperation between Russia and China—especially in the areas of artificial intelligence, cybersecurity, and space—has created a more formidable challenge to U.S. technological supremacy. China, with its rapidly expanding technological capabilities, poses a direct threat to U.S. dominance in sectors such as telecommunications, internet infrastructure, and digital finance. Meanwhile, Russia's sophisticated cyber capabilities, combined with its ability to engage in disinformation campaigns, have proven to be a major challenge to U.S. political systems. The collaboration between the two countries in these areas only amplifies the threat posed to U.S. global leadership in technology and security.

In conclusion, the Russia-China alliance represents a significant shift in global power dynamics, with profound implications for America's position on the world stage. As these two nations continue to strengthen their military, economic, and technological cooperation, the U.S. will face increasing competition in both its traditional spheres of influence and in emerging global domains. To maintain its global position, the United States will need to adapt its foreign policy and engage with this new geopolitical reality, balancing the need for cooperation with the strategic challenges posed by an increasingly aligned Russia and China. The emergence of this powerful alliance calls for a reevaluation of American strategies in both Europe and the Asia-Pacific, as well as a reassessment of its role in global economic and security institutions.

Conclusion

The strategic partnership between Russia and China represents a profound shift in global geopolitics, one that signals the decline of Western dominance and the rise of a new multipolar world order. Throughout this book, we have explored the various dimensions of the Russia-China alliance, including its military cooperation, economic synergies, and growing influence in global governance. What is clear is that this partnership is not merely a temporary tactical alliance but a long-term strategic alignment that is reshaping the global landscape in significant ways.

As Russia and China continue to deepen their ties, their collaboration will undoubtedly have far-reaching consequences for the balance of power across the globe. By leveraging their economic and military strengths, Russia and China are able to challenge the traditional dominance of the United States and its allies, offering an alternative model based on sovereignty, non-interference, and multipolarity. Their alliance has not only allowed them to challenge U.S. influence in regions like Europe, the Asia-Pacific, and the Middle East but also to reshape global trade, security, and technological systems in ways that prioritize their national interests.

For the United States, the emergence of this powerful alliance presents both a challenge and an opportunity. The U.S. must adapt to a new world where its dominance is contested, and where Russia and China's growing partnership will increasingly define the rules of global engagement. To maintain its relevance, the U.S. will need to rethink its approach to both economic and security policy, embracing strategic partnerships with regional powers, strengthening its technological edge, and seeking new avenues for cooperation with both Russia and China in order to manage global risks. The shift toward a more multipolar world offers an opportunity for the U.S. to reassert its leadership in global institutions, but it also requires a recognition that its role in the future of global governance will no longer be as the sole superpower.

Ultimately, the Russia-China alliance is not just a geopolitical phenomenon but a reflection of the evolving realities of a rapidly changing world. The future of international relations will be shaped by the ongoing dynamics between these two countries and their growing influence across all spheres of global activity. As we move forward, it will be essential to monitor how this partnership develops and how the U.S. and its allies respond to the challenge posed by a more assertive Russia and China. In doing so, we can better understand the path toward a new global order, where power is distributed more evenly among multiple centers of influence, and where the dynamics of competition and cooperation will define the next chapter of international relations.

www.ingramcontent.com/pod-product-compliance
Lightning Source LLC
LaVergne TN
LVHW061038070526
838201LV00073B/5093